Hampshire Hauntings and Hearsay

Mary and Ray with love — Patricia Ross

HAMPSHIRE HAUNTINGS AND HEARSAY

by
Patricia Ross

𝕿𝖍𝖊 𝕶𝖎𝖓𝖌'𝖘 𝕰𝖓𝖌𝖑𝖆𝖓𝖉 𝕻𝖗𝖊𝖘𝖘
1998

Hampshire Hauntings and Hearsay is published by
The King's England Press, 21, Commercial Road,
Goldthorpe Industrial Estate, Goldthorpe,
Rotherham, South Yorkshire
S63 9BL

ISBN 1 872438 18 0

Typeset in Perpetua by The King's England Press

Printed and Bound in Great Britain by
Woolnough Bookbinding
Irthlingborough
Northamptonshire

To the kind people of Hampshire and Sussex who have
shared with me their haunting stories

Nelson's famous flagship the Victory: *but is it haunted?*
[See page 9]

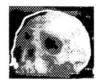

INTRODUCTION

I have never seen a ghost, but some people never do. There is, however, a strong belief that such beings exist and provide an explanation for the otherwise unexplainable. Some people tell me: "I don't believe in ghosts, but ..." and follow with a story of a personal experience for which they can provide no rational explanation. Many ghost stories appear to be fantasy or folklore, the result of the way someone felt at the time, hoaxes, misinterpretation of things half-seen in poor light or over-indulgence in another kind of spirit ... If, however, you accept that everything is possible, even if it goes against the laws of physics, then the world allows for the supernatural.

I accept ghost stories as the experience of the people who tell them, or as, more often, the reported experience of a friend of a friend (hearsay). Such stories may be vestiges of an old belief in life after death, left over from primitive times, oddly coexistent with or incorporated into more orthodox religion over centuries. For instance, there is evidence from early church art that some Saxon and Viking beliefs persisted well past the Norman invasion.

Some people have a lot of fun ghost-hunting and many books have been written about ghosts, especially those associated with turbulent and traumatic happenings. Whilst engaged in historical research, from time to time I have met haunting stories, told by apparently sensible, sincere people, some of whom were quite proud of their local phantom. Others were sceptical until the unexplainable occurred.

I could not have written this account without the help of the many people from Hampshire and nearby Sussex who have shared their paranormal experiences with me in letters to the King's England Press or in casual conversations. I have included some from the Isle of Wight and from parts of Dorset lost to the county in boundary changes. Stories continue to reach me; those for which there is no room here will be saved for a second volume. Please write to me if you would like to contribute.

Most of the ghosts I hear of are friendly to those who observe them or just peacefully coexist, harming no one. Some observers were scared at the time, but enjoyed sharing their stories. A few letters have reached me from people whose experiences are too personal or worrying to print here; I have suggested they contact the church or their medical adviser to obtain individual help and counselling. Anyone similarly worried may like to contact the Bishop of Portsmouth's office, Portsmouth Cathedral, as I gather from an article in The *News* of February 22 1995 that a priest has been appointed by the Bishop to advise and, if possible, to help people who believe they are troubled by spirits.

There is an ambivalence about the supernatural. I am not superstitious - am I? - but was caught absent-mindedly throwing spilt salt over my shoulder the other day.

"Why?" asked my husband.

"For good luck?" I said. " - Or to avert bad luck?"

"You are not consistent," he said. "I thought you didn't believe in that sort of thing."

"Of course I don't," I said; "But ..."

I am not going to go ghost-hunting; I'd frighten myself half to death. I present the following stories because I find them interesting, intriguing and - you never know, do you?

The Old Landport Gate, Portsmouth: Portsmouth has an abundance of ghost stories.

ARMED SERVICE GHOST STORIES

A feeling I was being watched.

It would not be surprising if there were ghost stories connected with Nelson's flagship, HMS *Victory*, on display in Portsmouth Dockyard. Mr. David Blackmore of Portsmouth, Quartermaster Sergeant (retired), Royal Marines, told me of his experience while serving as a boy bugler aboard the old wooden ship.

"You can't blow a bugle after an appendix operation," he began, "so I took over from a bugler who had had his taken out; and I used to practise bugling and drumming down below in the ship; it's set in concrete now ... It was very dull down there and you used to get shadows and a very creepy feeling. I used to be bugling or drumming away and had the feeling I was being watched and a cold shiver down my back. The hair used to stand up on the back of my neck and I'd feel cold - you'd look over your shoulder ... they used to say they had a ghost there. I acted as a guide and a bugler for about a year on the *Victory* and also looked after the visitors' bookstall."

Mr. Blackmore had a strange experience much later, when he was visiting war graves in North Africa. He took a photograph near one grave, because the name on it caught his eye; back in Portsmouth a lady whom his wife knew saw the photograph and recognised the name on the gravestone as that of her son.

"She had previously never found where he was buried."

The thud of boots pounding along ...

Aldershot has been the home of the British Army since 1854 when the War Department bought Aldershot Common and began to establish military camps there. An army runner was said to have been murdered by thieves while carrying the news to Aldershot of Wellington's victory at Waterloo in 1815, 29 years earlier. Brode writes that the thud of boots can be heard pounding along what is now Alma Lane, Aldershot, where he was ambushed, then they stop. The story has mysteriously slipped back in time because the army had not yet reached what was then a small hamlet at Aldershot. Alma Lane, Crondall, is claimed by Brookes to be haunted by a military messenger ghost, on the same errand, who was murdered by footpads. Are there two Alma Lanes, were two military messengers murdered (footpads were common enough in the early nineteenth century) or are these two versions of the same story?

Roman soldiers are said to haunt the area near the new Northam Bridge over the River Itchen near Bitterne Manor. Could their ghosts have been disturbed when the bridge was built, or was the haunting already there? I don't know. Do you?

Dumped in a well ...

At Lymington, earlier this century, Mrs Hamilton-Gordon of Bywater House was disturbed by doors opening and closing in the night. It was known that a supporter of Monmouth carried documents and valuables after the Battle of Sedgemoor to Bywater to hide until he met a courier who would take them to Holland. The plot was discovered, the young man killed and it is thought his body was dumped in a well. Mrs. Hamilton-Gordon believed his ghost wanted her to help him find the valuables. Later, inexplicably, a portrait print of her appeared to include a young man with Cavalier curls. The valuables were never found.

Royalist survivors retreated to the church ...

There are bullet holes in the wooden door of Alton's St. Lawrence Church, from a battle fought during the English Civil War when the town was a Royalist stronghold. It was attacked by Sir William Waller and his Parliamentary force in December 1643. After the Royalist cavalry had left (shame!), 500 Royalist foot soldiers faced a superior Roundhead force. Royalist survivors retreated to the church, defended it for over six hours but were overcome inside it. Their officer, Colonel Richard Boles, "slew with his sword six or seven of them (Roundheads) and then was slayne himself, with sixty of his men about him". (Epitaph in Winchester Cathedral.)

Dorothea St. Hill-Bourne has written that during one evening service in the church, she had a sense that she was surrounded by fighting soldiers. A local man assured her he knew of half a dozen people who on separate occasions had had the same weird impression. It has been suggested that an imprint of the battle somehow attached itself to the church. No one to my knowledge has whispered that, knowing of the battle, some observers may have dozed off in the sermon and misinterpreted sounds they heard as they awoke. It could easily have happened to me. However, it is widely believed that imprints of other battles are sensed by people now, for instance at Edge Hill.

A man in armour, on horseback ...

During the 2nd World War Alfred Crookes, returning to Crondall from a dance at Crookham, heard a knocking. As he went along Croft Lane by All Saints Church, Crondall, he was surprised to see a man in armour, on horseback, appear through the doors of Crondall Lodge. The horse carried its rider across the lane, through the churchyard wall and up an avenue of limes to the the church porch. Never again did Alfred pass the lodge after dark.

Military apparitions reputed to have been seen at Crondall church are thought to be echoes of battles fought in and around Crondall during the English Civil war. Was Alfred's horseman one of Waller's Roundheads, stationed in the village from 1643 while waiting to attack Basing House? The *Good Ghost Guide* says six Roundheads surrendered in Crondall and were put to death on 27 January 1645. Ghost-hunter Stephen Darby recorded his own observation in 1899 of a man in leather jerkin, armoured breastplate, black thigh boots and round helmet, who crossed the road and entered Crondall church-yard. He thought the man was dressed for a pageant, enquired and found there was none. The phantom soldier was seen by a number of local people from time to time.

The above stories are difficult to explain; the surprising aspect of them to me is that Cromwellian apparitions are accepted as commonplace in Crondall.

Colonel Norton

A Cromwellian military ghost, Colonel William Norton, is reputed to walk from the chine to the Old Manor House at East Wellow in the Romsey area. Stories of Cromwellian ghosts could have originated as a symptom of the Roundheads being deeply unpopular in formerly Royalist areas.

Ghostly pilots

The former Royal Aircraft Establishment, Farnborough, (now the Aerospace Division of the Defence Research Agency), boasts two ghostly pilots in and near its accident investigation hangar. If ghosts there be, this seems reasonable.

The ghastly remains of Jack The Painter (see story opposite)

On a stormy night ...

In life Jack Aitkin (Jack the Painter) worked in Portsmouth Royal Naval Dockyard. He started a fire in the dockyard ropehouse, was arrested at Hook Old Raven Inn, convicted of arson at Winchester, and hanged from the mainmast of the *Arethusa* in Portsmouth in 1777. It was believed at the time that he held anti-monarchist views and planned to blow up the fleet. Jack's body was hung in chains on the beach for years at Blockhouse Point, Gosport, as a warning to others, which is a macabre enough tale. Then sailors stole his body, loaded it into a sack and left it as pledge for a drinking debt at a Gosport pub. It is said that Jack's chains can still be heard on the Hard, Gosport, on a stormy night.

I can vouch for the fact that the story is alive and well as a number of people tried to persuade me I could hear Jack's creaking chains while we waited for a boat to a social event at one of the forts one wet and windy evening. Very eerie it was too, but I can't in all honesty say I heard anything but the wind and the slap of the sea.

Ran away screaming ...

Early in the nineteenth century, rumour had it that a weird apparition haunted the graveyard of St. Thomas's Church (now Portsmouth Cathedral) in High Street, Old Portsmouth. It was so weird that people who saw it ran away screaming. This was in the days when the local militia guarded Government House, the Governor's official residence. Even the guards were very frightened when they saw this figure leaping energetically in the churchyard opposite. It always appeared in darkness, was taller than a man and shrouded in white. It was seen by several people to leap from gravestone to gravestone and became known as Springheel Jack. The military tried to catch him by standing guard and laying traps, but never did.

This 'haunting' was a hoax perpetrated by a far from ghostly trickster who, in spite of the springs attached to his legs, nevertheless managed to slip away. The 'shroud' which covered the man and his metallic attachments was a bedsheet. To say he was unbalanced would hardly fit the bill. He was obviously sufficiently well co-ordinated to avoid slipping off gravestones. Mischievously mad, maybe?

13

Home of the R.M.L.I. ...

Forton Barracks, Gosport, was the home of the Royal Marine Light Infantry from 1848, contributing greatly to the town's prosperity until they marched away in the 1920's and the Royal Navy took over Forton as St. Vincent training barracks for boy sailors. Several ghostly stories are associated with the R.M.L.I.'s occupation of the barracks.

It came closer and closer ...

Soon after the R.M.L.I. took over, in the mid-1800's, on a particularly dark night a lone sentry was guarding the main gate at Forton when he heard the sound of a drum beating in the distance. As he listened, straining his ears, it came closer and closer. He peered into the night but could see nothing; nor could he see anything even when the sound of the beating drum came level with the main gate, then passed by to fade gradually into the distance.

The ghostly story was traditionally associated with the loss of life of a drummer boy in an epic battle of former times. He is said to have hung around his old barracks for some time, providing one-man drum displays over many years. The late Harry Camfield, who joined the red marines at Forton in 1914 as a 14-year-old boy recruit, confirmed, according to Ron Brown, that the ghostly drummer boy was heard during the early 1900's and that each time the guards were terrified. He seems to have moved out when the marines left Forton and has certainly not been heard since new housing development changed the town.

A weird, moaning sound ...

Another Forton Barracks ghost story concerns a nineteenth century sentry who actually saw and heard the ghost he described. He was on patrol at the rear of the barracks, which was at the time still fairly countrified, when he heard a rustling in the darkness together with "a weird, moaning sound". Two balls of light emerged from the gloom; they came closer as the moaning became louder. The sentry ran swiftly to the main gate where he collapsed and died of a heart attack shortly afterwards, so it's said. He must have been a city lad for the 'ghost' was no more than a friendly cow, the noise mooing and the lights a reflection in its big, sad eyes.

14

Strange noises in the night ...

Ghost stories, some much documented, attach to the Lower Quay area at Fareham, which was part of the old port. Some of the buildings there are preserved because of historical connections, and may have been used as a hospital treating injured sailors and later for keeping French prisoners of the Napoleonic Wars. This is the historical background to stories of vague hauntings, some of which may be connected with servicemen of long ago.

Unquiet spirits may, it was thought, have been disturbed when the area was used for light industry in the 1970's, for a workman at Palmers (light engineering) factory was frightened on night shift by a figure he said came through the wall, walked through the workshop and disappeared. At Miltalls (toolmakers and injection moulders) in 1977, a director's office lamp had, he said, "leapt into the air and floated about before it fell to the floor". Other Miltalls workers noticed tools moved to odd places, plugs which fell from sockets and strange noises in the night.

In ghost-hunters' jargon, two different phenomena were described here - a ghost and a poltergeist. The tools could have been misplaced by absent-mindedness or as a practical joke, but a rational explanation for the rest is difficult to find. I have recently heard, from a friend who spent time in hospital, that heavily sedated terminally ill patients have been known to experience images of people walking through walls: drugs or alcohol could explain some of the above.

Did sorrow cling? ...

After the Dieppe raid and D-Day landings in the 2nd World War, a former isolation hospital at Frater Lane, Gosport, was used as a mortuary for the bodies of soldiers brought ashore at Hardway. Did the sorrow experienced there cling to the place? For 25 years, murmuring voices and a sound of a scraping chair were heard in empty rooms and a shadowy figure passed across the floor on a sunless day, according to Fox.

Sick naval humour

The ghost of Fanny Adams, a nine-year-old girl murdered at Alton by Frederick Baker in August 1867, is said to appear in the former hopfield where the brutal deed took place. Frederick Baker, a clerk, was hanged for her murder at Winchester. Poor Fanny's name came to mean 'worthless' in naval slang, sailors having nicknamed canned meat, issued by the Royal Navy about the time of the girl's disappearance, 'Sweet Fanny Adams'. Yuk.

The grisly murder of Fanny Adams: a contemporary engraving from a 'Penny Dreadful'

GHOSTS OF THE ROAD AND RAILROAD

Famous headless lady of Ellingham

I have mentioned Lady Alicia Lisle's ghost in connection with the Eclipse Inn, Winchester (page 27). However, not only is she said to appear at the Eclipse, but also in the lanes near her former home, a sixteenth and seventeenth century building which was restored in 1870 and later used as a school at Moyles Court, Ellingham, near Ringwood. She appears in period costume, usually minus her head.

Another story relates how she travels by coach along the drive of Moyles Court to Ellingham church, drawn by headless horses and without a driver. She appears, it is said, complete with head (but held tightly beneath her arm like Ann Boleyn's was in the song about the Bloody Tower) at Dibden, where her son lived (near Hythe and at the edge of the New Forest).

Her crime was to have hidden two fugitives from the Battle of Sedgemoor, Monmouth's unsuccessful uprising. He was the natural son of Charles II and the opposition Whig party had pressed for his being offered the throne of England, prior to James II's accession. There was a lot of support for Monmouth in the South of England, and the brutal clamp down on his followers after his defeat was the Catholic king's reaction to the threat of long-term civil unrest by people who would strongly have preferred a Protestant monarch. The rebellion was neither well-organised nor successful, but must have seemed at the time to pose a considerable threat to the crown.

17

Ellingham is a lovely village, well worth a visit even if you fail to meet its famous headless lady. Lady Alicia in life used to sit in the canopied pew which now faces the pulpit in Ellingham church. After her execution she was buried in Ellingham churchyard, with her daughter. On each anniversary of Lady Alicia's death, a rose is placed on her tomb. Nobody knows how it gets there. I cannot help thinking that the more lurid of the Lady Alicia ghost stories may have been invented to heap insult on injury by a regime violently against Monmouth's supporters, and which harboured a particular resentment against her for being the wife of the man who signed Charles I's death warrant.

Ghosts of the old A3

The old A3, known as the Portsmouth Royal Road, provided a scenic journey in coaching days when travel from London to Portsmouth was neither as fast nor as comfortable as it is now. Travellers were bounced and vibrated towards their destinations in such vehicles as The Rocket, Clarke's Flying Machine, The Hero, The Regulator and The Nelson. Ron Brown of Fareham, local history enthusiast and writer, reminds me that long after the railways had made horse-drawn vehicles redundant, phantom coaches were seen on the London Road, sometimes (it is said) in the hours of darkness, surrounded by a ghostly glow.

Highwaymen, too, haunted the route: Claude Duval and Jerry Abershawe were well-known operators of this stretch of road. According to legend, Captain Jacques the highwayman was cornered by soldiers in room six of the Royal Anchor, Liphook, hid up a chimney to escape them and could not get down. He was either shot by the soldiers or perished up the chimney; his bones were discovered ten years later. His ghost is said to roam around on certain nights, so no one sleeps in that room. It is locked at night and used as a dressing-room during the day. Prisoners who were chained in the cellar (and in a blocked-off tunnel beneath the inn, which once ran beneath the old A3 to what is now a bank but was once another licensed premises) are also said to roam the inn from time to time. I wonder if they meet Captain Jacques?

A sailor's ghost was reputed to haunt the Portsmouth Road in the nineteenth century. It was associated in popular legend with a murder which occurred in 1786. The sailor was walking along the highway to

18

rejoin his ship when he was joined by three men also walking south, named Lonegon, Casey and Marshall. They were looking for work, but about level with the Devil's Punchbowl at Hindhead they combined to mug the sailor (to be precise, they slit his throat, took his money and clothes and rolled his body into the gorse). They were caught at Sheet near Petersfield , at a pub where they tried to sell the sailor's clothes. Not very subtle of them, was it? They were hanged for their crime and that was the last of the three villains. The sailor, however, mindful of his duty, could not rest and continued to try to join his ship, endlessly tramping along the Portsmouth Road. Many road ghost stories tell of phantom travellers to whom some misfortune occurred.

A one-legged man with a haversack full of Bibles ...

Fred Bason, an author, stayed in 1945 at Langstone. On his way from the Mill end of the village to catch a bus to Portsmouth one fine morning, he felt uneasy and everything went quiet. He wrote, for the *Saturday Book*, that he saw a naked man, bald, thin and with only half a right leg, lying in the road. The man vanished on his approach. He believed he had seen a ghost, drew what he had seen and sketched the apparition's position in relation to the road and village. What presence of mind! For a while he told no one, then wrote to the magazine to describe his experience.

Mr. Edward Greer of Havant read this story and contacted Mr. Bason; he told him he had seen the same figure in the lane five years previously, and had described it immediately afterwards at the Royal Oak as having a 'Duke of Wellington' nose. A stranger came into the bar who remembered a one-legged man with a crutch and a haversack full of Bibles who occasionally visited Langstone and had last been seen alive in 1932 or 1933. Pressed for a further description, he said the evangelist had "one of those aristocratic noses, thin and high in the middle". This tallied with Mr. Greer's memory. He showed the sketch he made at the time to Mr. Bason; it resembled Mr. Bason's sketch made during the 2nd World War, which he had shown to no one.

The water does not ripple ...

Bagwell Lane, Fleet, is said to be haunted by a White Lady. Some think she is the ghost of a woman drowned in a pond in about the

19

1880's. She is said to have appeared frequently, soon after the event. The haunting faded, then the lady was seen by a young motor cyclist (1968) who collided with the woman but felt no impact. Peter Underwood says many people have met this white-clad figure which appears and as suddenly disappears, and that although she seems to enter the pond, the water does not ripple.

Vanished before they could make contact ...

A young boy ghost who played the flute was described by a traveller on horseback in the 1800's. The horseman heard beautiful music, apparently coming from a tree on the road near Liphook. He thought it was heavenly music but later noticed a lad was walking beside his horse and playing a flute. After a minute or so, the horseman stopped to speak to the boy, who vanished. Several other people reported having seen this ghost, which always vanished before they could make contact, a habit ghosts seem to have.

The same story was told in about 1900: a horseman, who heard flute or pipe music coming from the top of a tree at Bramshott, realised that a fair-haired boy was playing the music whilst walking in front of the horse. A bramble twig momentarily knocked the rider's hat over his eyes; when he looked again, the boy was gone. Local people linked the apparition to the accidental death of a boy at the nearby mansion, Bramshott Court. Bramshott's spectral list includes two more horsemen (a Royalist soldier and a murdered highwayman); a potboy (from a stage coach?); a white calf which shrinks to the size of a bird when followed, then vanishes; a mother and her children; and a crowd of ghosts in sixteenth century costumes in Wolmer Lane.

They think they have run him over ...

Mrs. Eunice Longhurst of Southbourne, Bournemouth, says people she knows have seen the ghost of a tramp walking from the Straight Mile, Ampfield, towards Romsey. She writes: "They see him walking along the road in wet or foggy conditions. He walks into the road and they think they have run him over. When they stop to look there is no one in the road at all. This happened to my daughter's fiance twice, and we have heard of other people it has happened to."

The number of accidents hereabouts fell ...

A back seat ghost was seen in the rear-view driving mirror of a number of people along the Titchfield to Gosport via Stubbington road. It was first reported by an insurance salesman in 1979 near the old church at Crofton. Was it possible that the building of new housing estates disturbed it? The number of accidents hereabouts fell and the 'ghost' to whose appearance some of them were attributed appeared no more, after the road was straightened.

His bicycle lights went out ...

An Emsworth glazier told me that in about 1975 his brother-in-law, aged 16, who was cycling along a lonely bit of Hulbert Road (between Bedhampton and Waterlooville, where there are no houses to this day) when his bicycle lights went out. A car came up behind him and helped him along with its headlights.

"But you can guess what happened when he got to the end?" he said.

"It had disappeared?" I guessed.

"Yes, it wasn't there. He came home white as a sheet, you can imagine ... of course, it (the car) could have turned off, but there's nowhere to turn off along there, is there?"

I asked for his explanation.

"They say such things are ripples in time" he said.

A blinding light ...

A similar Hulbert Road ghost story was recounted to a friend, in June 1995, by the mother of a young man who was about 18 in 1974 or '75. The mother, now elderly, said that her son was on his motorbike, riding down Hulbert Road, when he saw someone whom he thought may need help, so stopped to give what assistance he could. He saw no one but there was a blinding light. He continued along the road and looked behind him in his driving mirror, in which all he could see was the light. No details are given in these two ghost stories of the sex, age or appearance of the 'ghost' behind the light or lights. I rather wonder if they spring from the same incident.

Joan was a neighbour and friend of Mrs. Evelyn Davis of Bedhampton, and also of an older lady whom I shall call Mrs.T. In about 1973, Mrs. Davis tells me, Joan told them both that she had been driving at dusk along Hulbert Road from Bedhampton towards Waterlooville with her son Steve, who was about 15 years old at the time. Hulbert Road used to be surrounded by quite dense woods before it was built up at the Waterlooville end as it is now. Anyhow, Steve said:

"Stop, Mum. There's a man flagging us down."

Joan had caught sight out of the corner of her eye of a figure in a long mac. She stopped. No one came to take the lift she was willing to offer, so Steve jumped out of the car to look for the person he had seen and she had glimpsed. He was puzzled because there was no one there.

"He must have run off into the woods," his mother suggested. But she thought the episode strange. When she told Mrs. Davis and Mrs. T. about the puzzling encounter, Mrs. T. said:

"My God, don't tell Steven. That's the ghost. It's famous for being seen there." Joan did not speak about it again to her son, because he was about to take his end-of-year exams and she did not want to worry him.

It was a good few years later that Mrs. Davis noticed a piece in the Portsmouth *News*. Either a little girl had written, or it had been reported, that she had done a school project on the area and had heard rumours of the ghost story, and that when the road layout was being altered, a skeleton had been found at about the place where Steve had seen the old man in the long mac. It was thought the remains were those of a tramp who had fallen in the ditch ... and that his spectral appearances were his cry for help and a proper burial. It was inferred that, as he was never seen after the bones were found, he was at rest, no longer needing to attract the attention of passers-by once he was decently buried.

Ghostly hitch-hiker

The following eerie tales also concern Hulbert Road but in each the ghost is definitely female.

Joan Forman writes that in November 1976, at dusk, Mr. and Mrs. Robert Spensley were travelling along Hulbert Road towards

Waterlooville on a stretch which had no footpaths. He was aware of a girl standing in their way so yelled to his wife, who was driving, to stop or swerve. She saw nothing, did neither and he closed his eyes, convinced they would run the girl down. The car hit nothing. There was no explanation.

Shaken, he told his workmates of the incident. They reassured him the "phantom girl" had been seen by other drivers from time to time, that she was a girl from Leigh Park who had been killed trying to hitch a lift to Waterlooville. Rumour said she had been hit by a car.

Another driver told of a girl who had flagged him down one stormy night near the cemetery in Hulbert Road and asked for a lift. He picked her up, concerned because she was so wet; he drove to the address in Leigh Park Estate she had given, turned to open the back door to let her out, and nothing was there but a very wet rear car seat!

A man from Data Heating, a firm which services boilers in people's homes, told me (1995) that the only ghost he had heard of in the Havant area was "the one in Hulbert road" whom a number of people had told him they had seen.

"Mind, I haven't seen her personally," he told me. "She's quite a modern girl who appears near the Hulbert Road junction with the motorway (the A3(M)), hitches a lift then disappears."
He had last heard of a sighting about five years before I spoke to him.

Two years later, a Havant friend told me he had heard a story that a ghost appears at Barton's Cross, which is between Emsworth and Rowland's Castle, on the Horndean Road not far from the car park of the BUPA hospital. The tale is of a girl who hitches a lift from motorists then vanishes. This is similar to the Hulbert Road ghost story above and concerns a site a few miles to the east of Hulbert Road; it is not too far, I should think, for an active lady ghost to commute, especially if she were provided with motor transport on request by kindly knights of the road. As the story is less detailed than the Hulbert Road one, I suspect that the story has migrated rather than the ghost, an example of hearsay which is passing into legend.

The phantom hitch-hiker is a popular ghost legend and I have heard of it recently connected with motorways. Rosemary Guille says that typically the girl is beautiful, often bedraggled. She gives her address, the motorist is always going that way; when she disappears she leaves something behind, e.g. a piece of clothing. The seat may still be wet where she sat. The legend is common in America, where it often continues with the motorist knocking on the door of the address he has been given, and there meeting the sorrowing parents of the girl on the anniversary of whose tragic death on the road the haunting incident occurred. He is shown her photograph; he goes to see her grave. If he has lent her his coat, he finds it hanging on her tombstone!

"Perhaps it came over with the Yanks," suggested an Englishman to whom I told this story.

Anything is possible with ghost stories. The phantom female hitch-hiker tales I have told above all refer to events since the war when American and Canadian troops were stationed in South coast areas of England. Canadians were camped in the woods at Rowland's Castle (not far from Hulbert Road as the crow flies) before D-Day.

One storyteller actually says the ghost is "quite a modern girl". (Leigh Park estate was built since the 2nd World War and the BUPA hospital is also a modern building.) I find it intriguing that so many stories are told about the same few miles of road; it is even more intriguing that the haunting story has shifted sideways a few miles. Could the following Hayling Story be connected? Perhaps not, but I was told (summer 1997) that a lady knocked over by a car on the bend of the main road into Hayling (by Smugglers' Cottage) "comes out onto the road from time to time. People in cars think they have knocked her down but when they stop to investigate there is no one there." Hayling Island is roughly eleven miles SSE of the Hulbert Road phantom hitch-hiker and eleven miles SSW of Barton's Cross.

It does not take long for ghostly traditions to take root and to become legend; for instance, construction workers tell stories about corpses walled into bastions of motorway flyovers.

An old newspaper-seller is said to haunt Redlands Lane in West Fareham, supposedly drawn back to the lane where he was murdered. No one remembers why or when.

At Hayling, the goods yard of the old railway station on the Hayling Billy line (a route cut by Beeching) is said to be haunted by a former employee of the railway. Mr Alan Bell, who represents Hayling Railway History with his model railway layouts of the Hayling Billy line, tells me that the ghost at the old Hayling station was thought to be that of Henry Wilkinson, a former signalman; it was last seen in a station building and reported in the Portsmouth *Evening News* both in 1963 and 1973. The station was converted into a theatre in 1996.

The Meon River at Droxford: a coach is said to plunge into the flood near this spot, in a terrible re-enactment of a tragedy from long ago [see next page].

They retraced their route ...

Mr. Gerald Durrant of Tuckton, Christchurch (which used to be in Hampshire) was driving along the Ringwood to Christchurch road with his wife on their way home from a folk festival in May 1995 when he saw "a monk-like figure" approach from near some big gates at the road side. He swerved violently to avoid a collision but it "passed right through the car" he said. He felt shaken. Asked to describe the figure, he said he could not see its face, it was "going too fast", but he drew the side view of a hooded person with a long spreading robe, a kind of kerchief beneath its chin, and in his first attempt at recall, what looked to me like a wimple (was it a nun rather than a monk?). His wife saw nothing and says there was no one in the road behind them; she confirms that her husband swerved at this point and is convinced he reported a genuine sighting. The following week they retraced their route and described the spot to a friend who recognised their description of some big gates as being at Bisterne, not far from the church. I wonder whether this may be connected to Mr. Clifford's story mentioned in the chapter "Monastic Hauntings" (page 39)?

Coaches and horses

Embley Park is said to be haunted by a ghostly coachman driving his coach and horses from the house to the church. At Westbury Manor, West Meon, now a residential home for the elderly, a phantom stage coach is said to travel across the grounds and a garden in front of the house. This story is linked with that of a murder in the road across from the house "years ago".

A ghostly coach and horses is said to hurtle down the drive of Hartley Mauditt's long ago demolished manor house. Bramdean reputedly has one which drives across the road. After a coach was wrecked and overturned in the river at Droxford, drowning its passengers, the incident was said to be supernaturally re-enacted on its anniversary for some years.

At Bentley, it is said a coach and horses phantom haunts the crossroads, and a ghostly monk crosses the A31. At Bramshott, Roger Newman, a local historian, was told in 1971 of the sound of a coach and horses heard along Rectory Lane.

The headless phantom of Lady Alicia Lisle, said to haunt the Eclipse Inn [See opposite]

SPIRITED INNS, HAUNTED HOTELS AND RESTAURANTS.

One could be less than serious about public house ghosts, for alcohol can lend a powerful spur to the imagination. On the other hand, some English pubs are centuries old. Their long history and ancient fabric encourage many a supernatural story, so if ghosts there be, where better to search for them? Hampshire has its share of spirited inns and haunted hostelries, with a restaurant or two for good measure.

A nice, tidy soul ...

It is said that the Miller's Pond, Sholing, Southampton is haunted by a ghost which "moves bottles about and reorganises things"; what a nice, tidy soul it must be! The establishment was formerly known as the Sholing Railway. It has been run by the same family, a father, then in 1988 his son, for more than twenty years.

After public outcry, her sentence was commuted to decapitation ...

One of the more spectacular Hampshire ghost stories is that of Lady Alicia Lisle who is said to haunt the Eclipse Inn, Winchester, in a top floor room where she lived before her execution. Her plight touched the hearts of those who knew her. Condemned by Judge Jeffries to be burned at the stake, her sentence, carried out in Winchester, was, after public outcry, commuted to the more lenient one of having her head cut off; there is more about her in the chapter "Ghosts of Road and Railroad" (page 17); the spectre of Lady Alicia gets about a bit.

It made me blink a bit ...

The Swan at North Warnborough is a heavily beamed old pub where General Waller's troops drank ale during the Civil War siege of Basing House. Not surprisingly, it is said to be haunted by three ghosts. Hearsay? I asked landlady Sheila Larner if it was truly haunted.

"Well," she replied; "it depends who you talk to. I don't really know. People say they've seen things after other people have been talking about it but it may be auto-suggestion. I have not really experienced much myself." Expecting a story of ghostly Roundheads, I asked what her experience was.

"Just a sighting of a woman - she could have looked like myself in a dressing-gown - coming downstairs. It was in the afternoon, not in the dark or at night or anything. I was not worried but it made me blink a bit. I was surprised but have never been scared here, even when I've been alone in the house."

Unexplainable behaviour ...

A story told to me by the publican at the 300-year-old Robin Hood on Rowland's Castle Green features his dog which, he says, howls outside a particular room, at "any time of the day or night". The room is empty. He was not complaining of ghosts; he thought the inn had none; he said, "I sleep too soundly for that, but the dog's behaviour is unexplainable."

No dog will go into the cellar ...

Sue Cobb, the landlady at the Brushmaker's Arms, Shoe Lane, Upham, has sent me details from a log book about the inn. She and her husband took over in June 1993. All the entries were written before that date, but they mention two ghosts.

"The pub is over 400 years old," she writes "so there must be at least a couple of ghosts! The ghosts are very nice and friendly, as we've never had a nasty experience.

"Last September, though, we did experience a couple of events during one particular week. The first was when we had friends to stay: they were in the bar after closing, as we were washing the glasses. A pint glass came off the shelf about two feet off the ground and landed on the bar's hard floor, with force, but it did not break or crack. Very strange! The second strange happening was when a mug came off the mug hooks in the kitchen and passed over the draining board to land three feet down on the hard floor of the kitchen, but it did not break or crack either. The hooks are like this (she drew a very curly shape designed to prevent accidental drop-off) so a mug's handle could not possibly just fall off."

The inn catered in the 16th century for a group of brushmakers who travelled the countryside to sell the new brooms they made of hazel sticks cut from hedgerows. Now, a certain brushmaker, named Chickett, made better brooms than the rest and sold at higher prices. He hoarded his profits, took them with him wherever he went, and hid them under his pillow in the little room at the inn where he slept. Here miser Chickett was murdered one night and his money taken, all but a gold coin or two which fell to the floor as his killers fled. Neither the murderers nor the money were ever found. It is thought the inn's ghost is either Chickett, spiritedly searching for his money; his murderer; or a former landlord who was murdered whilst counting his takings.

Guests who have stayed in the room have reported seeing a shadowy figure. Dogs have become restless, lain back their ears and growled, as if at something unseen. Local people are not keen even now to spend the night in the Mr. Chickett's room.

Upham School wrote a news sheet in June 1992, a page of which was sent to me by Mrs. Cobb. The young reporter had talked to the then landlady, 'Anne', who told her she had never seen the ghost but had seen many glasses move "without human help". So had one of her staff, named Dee, who had a bottle fly at her and smash in front of her. Shortly after that Dee left. (I don't blame her!) A barmaid named Diana had claimed to see the ghost as she was walking into the bar; she "saw a mist and a black arm pushed her backwards. Then the mist went away and she stood up." On Halloween, Anne, her husband Kevin, and Diana were talking when a black shadow passed over them. The school reporter was also told that no dog will go into the cellar where the former landlord was murdered.

The Royal Oak at Langstone is reputed to be haunted, some say by a lady who walks through walls, others say by ghostly smugglers. More about this in "Smuggling Connections" (page 67).

The pub had three ghosts ...

The George and Falcon on the A32 at Warnford is a large, one bar pub close to Old Winchester Hill and with the River Meon running through its garden. In March 1995 I was told by a woman who had lived all her life in the Meon Valley that it was reputedly haunted "by a woman whom a girl met on the stairs only everybody said there was no one there". The girl's "quite nasty experience" had been about two years previously. Of the ghostly lady, she added: "people see her and smell her". So the apparition had appeared to several people?

Mr. John Futcher, manager of the George and Falcon, said his pub had three ghosts which different people said they had seen. One was a lady all in white which a barman reported he had seen walk through a curtain; someone else saw a Cavalier looking through the window. Then, a few years ago, one of his cleaning staff reckoned she saw someone upstairs; "She got quite hysterical about it; she was minding her own business, cleaning on a Sunday. It was a shock, you see." (This was the incident I had heard of earlier.)

He did not know exactly when the pub was built, but it used to be The Falcon and was given the royal prefix after George III's visit on the way to Weymouth. Mr Futcher had not seen the ghosts himself; ("some people think they can see things, but who knows?" he said) and he did not know who the ghosts could be. However, a lot of people had stayed at the Falcon "when the big battle was on near Alresford" (the Battle of Cheriton, during the English Civil War of 1644, in which Royalists were heavily defeated by a Roundhead army led by General Waller); they (the Royalists ?) had stayed "in a barn round the back" (which might account for the Cavalier at least!).

The 'lovely young lady' on the landing

Mr. Fred Walker, landlord of The Original White Hart Inn, Ringwood, told me that his recently retired employee, Mrs. Freda Coombes, who had worked at the inn since she was twenty, had heard, from a long-retired chambermaid colleague at the inn, the story of a haunting on the corridor near room four. I 'phoned Mrs. Coombes, who told me the following story:

"A young man who was staying at the inn, just a youth - he had been there with his mother and had stayed on for a few days on his own, I think - asked the older maid, who was doing the breakfasts as

30

usual:

'Who is that lovely young lady I was talking to in the middle of the night? Is she the landlord's daughter?'

"Well, the landlord had no daughter and there was no young female guest at the time. He had seen the 'lovely young lady' on the landing, seated on a laundry basket in crinoline clothes at the end of the corridor and spoken to her briefly, just to wish her goodnight I think - he was just a young lad. She had not replied to his greeting and he had not realised the lady was a ghost.

"The girl who worked there saw it (the apparition) two or three times herself" added Mrs. Coombes. "She seemed genuine enough; just sensitive to such things. For instance, there used to be a slaughterhouse in Ringwood opposite the Granary , between the two banks. She used to go home down another lane a longer way round, rather than pass it, for she said she heard horses' hoofs following her down there! She can't have known about the slaughterhouse, which had gone long before then."

A gentleman who keeps opening a wardrobe door ...

Mrs. Roberts of Ringwood tells me a lady walks the corridor of the Crown Inn, Ringwood, "quite regularly". Although she has not personally seen the apparition she has "heard of people who have seen her, in an old-fashioned long dress and a black robe. She looks like a housekeeper or something." There is also supposed to be a gentleman, she says, at the same inn, who keeps opening a wardrobe door; "I put that down to the flooring" she adds. "It doesn't worry guests".

Is it a trick of the light? ...

At Chalton, the Red Lion dates from the thirteenth century and claims to be Hampshire's oldest pub. It had a regular knocking sound on Saturdays near its chimney breast, variously explained as something paranormal or something happening at another building, heard through a chalk vein on which both buildings stand. Some say a phantom horse and cart are driven fast across the road from the Red Lion down a small hill; others say it is a trick of the light reflected on roadside puddles!

31

Julie's Restaurant, High Street, Emsworth, is a former fisherman's cottage, about 300 years old. Within the building is the filled-in archway of what is believed to be the entrance to a smugglers' tunnel. The restaurant is reputed to be haunted, some say by a ghost woman. The proprietor, Mr. K.M. Hartley, who has been at Julie's since March 10 1993, told me he had not personally seen anything supernatural in the place but there was definitely "something unexplained". Most of the strange occurrences happened before he took over; however, he has smelled a strange, musky smell.

"The first time I walked into the building, I smelled it," he says; "it was like walking into an attic and opening an old box. It was just in part of the restaurant, near the back, upstairs on the restaurant floor. I've had the same experience twice more; and I don't drink or smoke or anything. There's a flat upstairs which is unoccupied; we've had customers get up from their chairs when they heard footsteps, to let someone through from the flat door. They've been very surprised when we told them there was no one there. The immediately previous owners, the Ellacombes, also had customers at table two, who got up to let someone through from the flat ..."

Mr. Hartley had been told that Julie, the original owner of the restaurant and a former actress, had "seen something". And Mr. Ellacombe "used to employ a commis chef who saw a face outside in the holding area, but I only have garbled information about that. But what really convinced me was the stick of celery on the meat hook ..."

"What stick of celery?" I asked.

"Well, it was hanging on a meat hook," he repeated. "There are only two chefs and we know each other well. It's not the sort of thing we'd do"; (celery belongs in a vegetable rack and meat on a meat hook, definitely).

" ... Neither of us put the celery there, no one else could have put it there, but there it was! It's only happened once ... there have been physical things, like we've been in the kitchen and a door has slammed; it could have been the wind, but there wasn't much wind; or a door which is usually closed will suddenly open. Then there was the time when I was working here alone on a Saturday night. It was about 1.00 a.m. and I was very tired, but I had to keep on working to prepare for a big party the next day. Now, Emsworth is a very windy place but can be very mild. This night was very quiet. Suddenly the back door shut with an almighty force and I knew there wasn't any wind.

"I won't disbelieve anything, but most of the strange happenings concern physical things, like the celery and the door … my mother would say she could sense some thing when she lived in the flat. Once a member of staff was cleaning the restaurant and the Hoover turned itself off on its own! If there is something there, it's more apparent when someone sparks it off. We employed an eighteen-year-old once; told her about the ghost and it frightened her silly. More happened when she was there for a week than at any other time! Sometimes you wonder whether people sense things just because they know the place might be haunted," he mused. "For instance there was a sack of onions on top of the stairs the week the previous owners left. Mrs. Ellacombe was telling people about the ghost and maybe the onions were unsettled or something. They toppled down the stairs and the people there were frightened stiff; and it was only onions!"

Mr. Hartley added that his mother said she "saw something" in the living room of a neighbour's house, which the neighbour claimed was haunted. It was only when his mother described what she had seen that Mr. Hartley remembered having seen the same figure which he had thought was a brown statue. There was no statue in the room; so if it was a ghost, he had seen one without realising it.

Under the influence or not?

Alton's Crown Hotel (*circa* 1660) has timbers stripped from old warships in Hampshire dockyards. When gales blow from the sea it is said the cries of sailors and wind howling through the rigging can be heard.

The Crown's female ghost, possibly a serving maid, is more often sensed than seen.

I asked the present manager, Mr. David Hale, if he knew of any hauntings at the Crown. He replied:

"You mean about the dog? (see animal chapter, page 75) Not since I took over a few months ago."

I said I'd read about the dog … when was the last time anyone had noticed anything?

"Under the influence or not?" he asked.

"You tell me" I said.

He said the previous manager, Mr. Keith Reeves, whom he

assured me was not "under the influence", had noticed something about a year previously (1994). Mr. Hale thought it was howling. He had possibly felt something but not seen anything. There was a room upstairs, though, where people had seen a funny old lady in white, which was more possible. They had found out afterwards that someone had died in that room.

It was the lady; I could see her against the light from the window ...

A gentlewoman, possibly a nursemaid, is said to watch children at play at Buriton. I wonder whether there is any connection between her and a female apparition Mr. John Ligertwood, landlord of the Five Bells, Buriton in 1995, told me about:

"There is a little old lady who has been spotted in the pub," he told me. "I've seen her a couple of times in the morning, going up the steps between the restaurant and the lounge bar, and also she's been in the bedroom.

"I thought she was my cleaning lady, Edna ... but the woman was only four feet tall and Edna is nearer six feet than four feet; anyhow, Edna was somewhere else in the pub at the time and hadn't seen anyone.

"It was not an old lady you could touch ... Edna once saw her, too, in the public bar. She said to me: 'I'll leave you to your friend' but there was nobody there! She described exactly what I had seen the first time I saw the old lady, at about 9.30 one morning. She wore a definite head-dress and peasant-type clothing: a full skirt, heavy, in a cross between linen and hessian and a shawl or headscarf. It was about four years ago; I don't remember all the details.

"But shortly afterwards, I was in my bedroom; I had a chest of drawers in there and I heard someone in the room. Now, my family were living with me at the time and there was a kind of freeway through the room; you know, anyone who wanted a pair of socks or anything would come and rummage in my chest of drawers. But it was the lady; I could see her against the light from the window. I shouted at her: 'What do you want?' and she went. I'm telling you, I got goose pimples and my hair stood on end. I've not seen her for three years now."

"When you say 'she went', do you mean she walked out, drifted out or disappeared?" I asked.

"I'm not sure; it's a long time ago now ..."

He added a further story that may or may not be connected with the above. One Sunday evening, as he sat in the lounge with his girl-friend, having decided to have one glass of wine before going to bed, the door, which he had just closed, came open and a sensor light came on.

"They are susceptible to temperature and I felt a bit eerie," he went on. He mentioned this to his companion.

"I'm going home!" she said.

He told her he was only joking but felt a chill wind from the open window.

"I had to switch on the lights," he says; "the little latch on the door can't possibly open on its own."

He emphasises that he has never seen anything or heard anything eerie when he has had more than an odd glass of wine, although he does sometimes drink with customers ("it's part of the job"), and that different people have felt different atmospheres. Customers have said that the lounge bar was busy, e.g. "There's an awful lot of people in there now!" when there were none. He has sat downstairs with staff after closing time, to relax after a busy week-end, when they had all heard "a burst of noise like a party you know, hundreds of people having a ball; it was quite unnerving. The atmosphere was peculiar but there was nobody there."

A man seen hurrying from a room ...

An obelisk on Clarence Pier, Portsmouth, marks the place where John Felton, who murdered the Duke of Buckingham in 1628, was displayed in chains. The old Spotted Dog inn, where the crime took place, was said to be haunted by the sounds of murder and a man in seventeenth century garb, seen hurrying from a room.

Brode and Farquharson-Coe each write of a ghost said to be that of a sailor who died as the result of being hit with a pewter pot during a fight between sailors and marines at the former Blue Posts Inn, Portsmouth. The inn was burned down in 1870 and rebuilt but appears to be no longer there. In the new building, sightings were reported of a man in seventeenth or eighteenth century sailor's costume with a bloodstained kerchief. One guest got up in the night to complain to the management that the fellow was sharing his bed; when, however, he returned with a member of staff to have the 'ghost' evicted, the bed was empty; no one was to be seen. One wonders how much convivial spirit the aggrieved guest had had to drink the previous evening and whether his ghostly companion snored.

The Press Gang at one's heels

Ron Brown tells how, 200 years ago or so, it was not always safe to pop into one of the many Portsmouth pubs for a pint for, should an impromptu visit be paid to it by the Press Gang, one might well be invited to go on a long, unplanned sea cruise. Pubs could, however, provide a welcome refuge, should the Press Gang be at one's heels; many Portsmouth pubs and beerhouses in those days had sliding panels with a secret room behind where fugitives could take refuge, then emerge safely to drink another day. However, less scrupulous landlords would sometimes slip into their secret rooms when all was quiet to slit the fugitives' throats, to take valuables and to dispose of bodies. Such incidents sparked off ghost stories, in which the victim came back from the dead to haunt the public house in question.

The town had the reputation once of containing more pubs and beerhouses for its size that any other in the land, to cater for sailors ashore. The story is told of an unidentified pub in East Street, Portsmouth where a foreign sailor was 'chatting up' a local girl in the corner of the bar; in an argument about the girl, he was knifed by a drunken British seaman. The seaman's shipmates immediately gathered round and, by the time the law enforcement officers arrived, all evidence of the skirmish, including the knifed corpse, had been removed.

For many years afterwards, landlords and staff of the beerhouse reported ghostly sightings and sounds made by the victim, who was always dressed as a seafaring man. When the beerhouse was being demolished in the 1890's, workers removed an old fireplace behind which they found a nook containing a skeleton dressed in seaman's clothing.

A fluffy grey, cat ...

The Guardsman, in Fratton Road, Portsmouth, an eighteenth century coaching inn, is reputed to be haunted by a beautiful lady's friendly spirit, who floats along corridors and through walls quite frequently. Its other ghost is supposed to be a little boy who holds a fluffy grey cat. Childish laughter is heard from a room which is, of course, found to be empty when you open the door.

King Charles I stayed in Andover at what became the White Hart hotel; the building is reputed to have at least three ghosts: a tall woman who walks about upstairs, and vague shapes of a man and a woman who drift about.

Ghostly shoves in the back ...

Opposite Matthew Noble's statue of Lord Palmerston in Romsey Market Place stands the Palmerston bakery and restaurant. Staff, who have been startled by ghostly shoves in the back, strange noises and lights being switched on and off, refer to the perpetrator of these anomalies as Charlie and believe that he inhabits the boiler room and attic. Eccentric electrics and poor plumbing? Maybe; but what about the shoves in the back? Nothing untoward has been reported for some time.

The landlord of the Baker's Arms, Droxford, told me his staff said there was a ghost in his 1745 pub that "keeps tapping them on the shoulder. There's a shadow. I think it's a monkey," he added, with a charming smile. I doubt if he were serious but he might have been. Ghostly taps on the shoulder are not far removed from the shoves in the back in the previous story and equally unexplainable (unless a practical joker was at work). But the monkey? Believe that or not as you will, dear reader. I have a feeling I was having my leg pulled.

Old-fashioned nursery rhymes ...

Simon and Lindsey were the new landlord and landlady of the White Hart at Cadnam when I spoke to Lindsey one evening in April 1995.
"We've only been here since July," she told me. "There's been a major renovation going on; but I said to a customer just recently, 'I think this place has a presence.'
"He said: 'Well, it has. Haven't you heard the stories?'
" 'No,' I said; 'but I felt, well, you could be at the bar and you'd think there was someone waiting to be served and there would be no

one there.'

" 'You're not the first person to feel that,' the man said.

"Then there's the story of a child upstairs and the lady who used to come into the room at night and recite all the old-fashioned nursery rhymes. The child would recite these old rhymes and the parents would say 'where did you learn that one, then?' and the child would say 'From the lady who keeps me awake at night; she sits on the end of my bed and tells me nursery rhymes.' "

Spirits or inspired by spirits ...?

Mr. James Kidd, proprietor of the Compasses Inn, Damerham, listed five ghosts which reputedly haunt his premises: an old lady, a baby, a young man, an old-fashioned lady and a coach and horses. The old lady ghost gently rocked in the attic in a ghostly rocking chair; she and a phantom baby heard in the attic had been experienced by a female member of staff in about 1992, who said they were friendly ghosts. "She was sensitive to that sort of thing" said Mr. Kidd.

Also, there was a man "who put his fiancee on the Titanic and cut his throat when he heard that the ship had sunk; an unnecessarily dramatic ending, but there it was". The previous owner of the inn had told him this story and had personally seen the ghostly chap in what was now Mr. Kidd's bedroom. The only experience Mr. Kidd himself had had of this nature was that of a door, on automatic closure in this bedroom, which had opened by itself and stayed open for 20 or 30 seconds when it should have closed automatically.

"You could say it was a draught or something," he said, "but it was very strange."

"And the other two?" I prompted.

"A coach and horses drifts from the old coach house, now a garage, and across the yard; and a young lady in an old-style dress is supposed to drift across the car park", he told me.

"The only thing is," he added, "when you are at a pub, you never know whether these stories are of spirits or inspired by spirits, if you see what I mean."

Quite.

A story about the Cottage Bar at Abbot's Ann appears in the chapter "Smuggling Connections" (page 67).

MONASTIC GHOSTS

Hauntings by phantom monks are reported throughout these islands. Real monks' wanderings after the Dissolution of the Monasteries in Henry VIII's time may have given rise to ghostly legends or, alternatively, the dispossessed monks may have died in difficult circumstances or taken up other callings out of necessity, then ended up unable to reach the next world or at least slipping in and out of the hereafter somehow. Could this happen? The Dissolution provoked a huge social upheaval in the land. Either explanation is possible, depending on your point of view.

Cistercians at Beaulieu

King John is said to have inaugurated the building of Beaulieu Abbey after a particularly vivid dream. He endowed it richly and admired the work in progress. Its dedication was in the presence of his son (Henry III), his queen and their entourage. Cistercian monks formed its community until the abbey was dissolved by Henry VIII.

The village's monastic ghosts, especially lay brothers dressed in brown habits, reputedly wander the countryside near Beaulieu. A monk was seen pruning a vine in the modern vineyard in 1979, so a visitor said. This may be the lay brother reportedly seen peacefully tending the land by a number of people over the years. A lady in 1927 was walking her dog at dusk when she was shown where to dig by what is thought may have been this same lay brother; a box containing stones and bones was found there. One account says she ensured the bones had Christian burial, after which ghostly chanting was heard. Ghostly chanting heard in Beaulieu is said to be associated with a local death.

Farquharson-Coe writes of the museum curator at Beaulieu having heard a ghostly funeral party at what used to be the abbey graveyard (the monks are understood to have buried their dead at night). Specifically, he heard footsteps, thuds and metallic clinks, which he thought could have been made by digging. One night in 1959 he heard chanting through his cottage window. This story does not, however, mention a death other than that implied in connection with the ghostly funeral.

Special Operations

The Special Operations Executive which trained agents to be dropped in Nazi occupied Europe during the 2nd World War occupied houses on the manor estate in the village; several of these student 'spooks' are said by Brode to have seen Beaulieu's ghostly lay brothers, which were so commonplace in the village they were accepted by locals as part of the community.

It occurs to me that ghost stories could have been perfect cover for the appearances and disappearances of those brave men and women engaged in Special Operations. Brode wrote that 50 years ago (the war years) the vicar, the Rev. Powles, used to hold a midnight mass for Beaulieu 'ghosts' on Christmas Eve. Was he really "on good terms with ghosts", as Miss Elizabeth Varley, who knew him, has said? Or was he colluding in innocent wartime deception? The patriotic slogan 'Careless Talk Costs Lives' was known to all, and a well-placed word about a haunting would have seemed a harmless enough rumour to pass, possibly confusing to enemy Intelligence.

The abbot was a considerable nuisance ...

Beaulieu ghost stories are of busy, benign beings, except for the Abbot Hugh, described by Joan Grant in *The Winged Pharoah*; she also describes her belief in and experiences of previous incarnations, one of which was in Ancient Egypt. She was married for a while to the late Mr. Charles Beatty, first Curator of Beaulieu Motor Museum, who admitted that he found her involvement with the ghostly abbot a considerable nuisance.

A former monastery

Now a furniture showroom, Broomhill Manor at Cove, Farnborough, is believed to incorporate some late thirteenth century building work in its structure, some claim from a former monastery on the same site. A phantom monk is said to haunt the house. A chapel at Christchurch priory church is said to be haunted by a monk.

Winchester ghost stories

One might have supposed that, if turbulent historical events produce hauntings, Winchester would be full of Arthurian knights (or were they only legendary?) or of argumentative Cavaliers and Roundheads (who definitely weren't); however, the only recorded apparitions there, of which I have read or been told so far, are of monks and nuns and a man in black who may have been a priest.

Monks and nuns in procession have reputedly been seen from time to time near the Royal Hotel (supposed to be on the site of a former convent); a limping monk was frequently seen by a canon's wife in the garden of one of the Close houses; it was reported in 1962 that he would glide through a wall into the cathedral and was never seen again after the wall was pulled down. Of three skeletons discovered, one was found to have arthritic changes which might have caused a limp. (From their date of death, it was deduced that they could have been members of a monastic order.)

Another monk, thought to be a Benedictine one, was said to haunt a track to Compton from Winchester; Benedictines are known to have held land in the area, which is now covered with housing estates. Since they were built, no one has seen the monk. It is noticeable that haunting reports often start or finish with building work or demolition on the 'haunted' territory, as if something is shaken up to allow us a peek into another world or to let the ghost slip away to where it belongs.

A priest, the Rev. Ramsdale Whalley, incumbent of Holy Trinity, was called in to exorcise something strange and uncanny in a house in Quarry Road, Winchester, where Mrs. Bowles and her husband Ronald lived from 1967. The couple both worked at Winchester railway station. She said she had seen a nun, a woman in white and a man in a black, high-collared coat with brass buttons, who smiled and stood back; his appearance was accompanied by a musty smell. Voices had called her name, usually before a death in the family. Her husband had seen nothing but noticed inexplicable movements of objects in the house. Mrs. Bowles said the 'ghosts' became more frequent each time an exorcism took place (hardly what one would expect).

Did not realise it was a ghost...

Miss Clare de Hamel, a retired probation officer who worked in Portsmouth from the early 1940's, now lives in Southsea. She told me, in February 1995, that she believes as a child she saw a ghost but did not realise it was one until much later.

A gentleman in a brown dressing gown ...

"We lived in Winchester then; it would have been in approximately 1929. We lived in a fairly modern little house in St. James's Lane. I was a Protestant child (although she later became a Roman Catholic) and because of the family's background they were very anti-Catholic at the time, so I certainly knew nothing about Catholics whatever," (and therefore knew nothing of monks).

"One night I woke up, probably only about ten or 11 o'clock, because my father was still dressed when I called him; walking through my bedroom out of the window was what I thought was a gentleman in a brown dressing gown - I wasn't frightened, oddly enough; I called my father and told him what had happened and he was very: 'oh, yes, well, these things happen'. It was only as a grown-up, when I went to stay at Mount St. Bernard's Abbey in Leicestershire, which is Cistercian, that I realised that it was a perfectly good Cistercian monk that walked through my bedroom. But it was interesting because, as I say, I'd never seen a Cistercian monk in my life ... I would have been about ten."

"You are absolutely convinced that it was a ghostly monk?" I asked.

"Well, he ... I mean, he walked through a bedroom window on the first floor ..."

"So ... he must have flown or something?"

"Well, exactly ..."

"It's interesting that you weren't at all scared ..." I said.

"Wasn't it?" she agreed.

"So if it was a spirit it must have been a kind spirit?"

"Yes, that's right."

Rather a nice ghost story ...

She had had no similar experiences, but told of a family friend who had, one of a married couple who lived in a house called Friar's Barton, in Winchester, she thought in Jury Street. She was not sure of their surname but they were of "an old county family" well- known in ecclesiastical circles. When the wife was nursing her desperately ill husband, every night at about 3 o'clock in the morning a monk would go through the room, looking absolutely miserable. One day she asked him if she could do anything to help him but he shook his head. About a week later the dean rang her up and said that they'd been looking at the foundations of the cathedral "because for the umpteenth time they'd flooded; they'd found a bulge in the wall which they had opened, and in it was a walled-up monk, who for about five minutes was absolutely perfect; his fingernails had gone where he had been trying to get out but otherwise he was completely perfect, because of course the air hadn't got to him, and then he crumbled to dust so ..."

"And was this at exactly the same time that she had had these ghostly experiences?" I interrupted.

"It was while her experiences were going on, yes: so she asked the dean what he was going to do with the dust and he replied:

" 'Oh, well, we'll put it in a museum.'

"So she said: 'No, you jolly well won't. It's a Christian man; you give him a Christian burial!'

"I mean, okay, he had a Church of England funeral and he was obviously a Roman Catholic, they did the best they could; and the day after the burial, which she'd gone to, of course, he (the ghostly monk) again appeared, but looking happy; he just raised his hand and blessed her and she never saw him again ... which is rather a nice ghost story, isn't it?" She added that I'd better check the story from another source as this was only hearsay from a tale heard in her childhood.

Link in the chain is tenuous indeed...

In an attempt to verify the above story, I consulted the County Library at Winchester and learned that during the eighteenth century the crypt floor was covered with almost five feet of earth to absorb flooding. Canon F. Busby, in *Winchester Cathedral 1079-1979* writes of an interesting discovery made when the original level was recovered during alterations soon after 1896. Under the east wall of the Lady Chapel a lead coffin was found, built up with brick and stone. Six feet long, the coffin had on it a plain Latin cross at the foot of which was the shield of the arms of the Courtenay family. Now, the place of burial of Bishop Courtenay, who died on 2 September 1492, had been lost. It seemed very likely that the body was his, especially when the remains of the funeral pastoral staff were found associated with it. The burial was above water level and could possibly have been left where it was but it was thought preferable to move the tomb carefully and to give it a more prominent burial. The cross and the Courtenay arms were set in a new ledger stone and a new monument was put in the south east corner of the cathedral quire near the altar rails.

It was not the first time a cathedral tomb had been moved. For instance, the Rufus Tomb was moved twice in the nineteenth century, the last time in 1886, to beneath the tower, where according to tradition Rufus was originally buried. But by then experts agreed that the person in the tomb was probably not Rufus at all but an unknown, important ecclesiastic, as Rufus's bones are mixed with those of Canute in a mortuary chest.

The above two paragraphs illustrate that it has not always been easy to decide what it was suitable to do when a body was found or to establish its identity, and that there was discussion at the time that the coffin was found in the Lady Chapel on both counts. The flooding, the finding of the body, and the discussion prior to reburial of the body believed to be that of Bishop Courtenay, who was possibly a member of a monastic order, all echo aspects of Miss de Hamel's walled-up monk story.

The information from the library also shows that tradition does not always represent known fact. Miss de Hamel heard her walled-up monk story when she was young, the source being family friends who may have been contemporary with or probably older than her parents, but it is not clear from her story or in her memory just when the reported incident took place. As she was a child in the early part of the twentieth century, the story she heard could have concerned real events in the late part of the nineteenth. Could the sad then smiling monk apparition, therefore, have been that of Bishop Courtenay? And whether or not it was, how could one explain the state of the

Carisbrooke, forever associated with the doomed Charles I

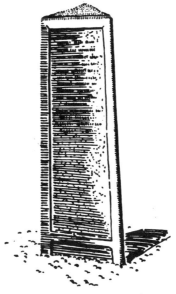

The Rufus Stone, standing at the spot where William met his strange
nemesis

fingernails in the walled-up monk story? My husband suggested to me that in the days when matters medical were less well understood than today, a stupor or trance might have been mistaken for death, which could have led to a person being buried alive in error; well, one would scramble like anything to get out if one awoke to find such an error had been made, wouldn't one? Too far-fetched a theory by half, I told him.

We will never know the truth now, and the missing link in a chain of evidence which connects the apparition to the historical event is tenuous indeed. It may indeed link to a different historical event, or to nothing tangible at all. The Winchester Museums Service found nothing about a walled-up monk in the sites and monuments record for the city, nor had the City Archaeologist's department heard mention of such a discovery during a recent project in the cathedral's crypt. My enquiry was passed on to the curator to the Dean and Chapter of the Cathedral, from whom I have had no reply.

Incidentally, according to Rosemary Guille, it was common in the Middle Ages for nuns to have their cells bricked up, leaving a small window for receiving food. (Barbaric!) Legends survive of nuns having been bricked-up alive having broken their vows, but I have not heard of a walled-up monk except in Miss de Hamel's story.

He didn't know they were ghosts ...

Miss de Hamel talked to one the monks at Buckfast about ghostly experiences and asked him how they "fitted in". The Buckfast monk had replied that, as there was no time in eternity, it could well be that 'ghosts' had got to come back until they found somebody kind.

"You know, that could have been their sort of punishment for something they'd done, and you can't say that it's three hundred years later or two hundred years later because there isn't any time ..."

It was the best explanation she had heard. She added, as an example of someone seeing a ghost without knowing that it was one, that she had been told that one of the Buckfast monks (a real one) had been to a Dartmoor farm in his capacity as parish priest, to see some Irish servant girls ... this was Devon, not Hampshire, but it was relevant ... the owner of the farm, who was not a Catholic (so it was assumed knew little about monastic orders), gave him something to drink and told him:

"I often used to see your monks when I was a boy."

The Buckfast monks, Miss de Hamel went on, wear black; so Father John said: "Did you, when was that?" because the farmer was an old man and the time of his youth would not have fitted in with when the black monks had come back to Buckfast. The farmer mentioned an approximate date, which was twenty years before the date of their return to the abbey. He said he never saw them after that because his father, who had had the fishing rights on the river Dart, subsequently gave them up, so he never went back. So Father John asked what the monks he had seen were wearing. The farmer replied that they were wearing white.

"Well, of course," added Miss de Hamel, "the pre-Reformation monks who were there did wear white; he'd seen ghosts; he didn't know they were ghosts but he had! He thought they were real monks, so he had no idea he was telling a ghost story.

"They are nice stories aren't they, not vengeful stories?" she added.

Phantom footsteps ...

At Buriton an underground passage led from the manor to the church. Phantom footsteps were heard going one way only! A spectral monk is said to have been seen by a number of people to walk up and down the main street according to Underwood; another, dressed like a priest, has been seen in the manor grounds. We didn't meet either of them on the two occasions we visited the seventeenth century Five Bells pub restaurant in the High Street; excellent meals both times, but no ghosts.

Netley Abbey is said to be haunted by monastic ghosts, one of whom is an abbot telling his beads. A skeleton found in a wall cavity in 1750 was alleged to be that of a bricked-up nun. There is more about Netley (page 73) in the chapter "Smuggling Connections".

Ghostly monks appear in the story told about Arreton manor (chapter on houses page 53) and Mr. Gerald Durrant recently reported seeing a monk or nun in Bisterne (page 17 "Road and Rail" chapter) which bore a striking resemblance to the parachutist/nun described next.

The apparition in the Bisterne story may be connected with or even be the same as that Mr. R.E. Clifford described seeing as a boy at "a large country house near Christchurch". Brode, who tells the story, does not specify which country house it was.

Mr. Clifford was 13 at the time (August 1941), and was staying at the house after being bombed out from his home in Southampton, when he and a friend saw "a shrouded white figure, about 5ft 8in tall" at the end of the veranda. They thought it looked like a nun, so assumed it was a German paratrooper in disguise. This made sense at the time for we were all on the look-out for enemy parachutists after the fall of France; there had been reports that paratrooper /nuns had been used by the enemy to infiltrate France and the Netherlands and warnings had been given that it might happen here. So, anyhow, the boys noted the 'nun' did not appear to be armed, bravely crept up to within a few feet of it, and fled when they noticed it was slightly floating and had no face!

Old bow-fronted house on the A3 at Petersfield. Is the A3 Hampshire's most haunted road? [See page 17]

STRANGE PERSONAL EXPERIENCES

Mrs. Davis of Bedhampton has occasionally had premonitions. Once, she approached a house where she had always been well received and had the feeling: "I know when I get to that house there'll be trouble." There was. (I have been told the nature of the trouble, but not for publication.) Another time, she says, she knew a child in the family was ill. She saw her aunt walk towards her but could not see her face.

"I just knew that he had died," she said. "Then my aunt told me he was dead."

Bones of Roman soldiers

Mrs. Davis had always hated Scratchface Lane, Bedhampton, in the same way that she felt Hulbert Road, when she was a child, was "creepy". She tells me that when the Broadmarsh Roundabout was being built (near the start of the A3M), bones were dug up at the end of gardens in Scratchface Lane. Experts, she had heard, were convinced they were the bones of Roman soldiers, because the Roman Road had run right through from Havant, very straight. The bones had been interred, she believed, with a little ceremony.

Had her feelings of disquiet in the lane been a sixth sense that the Roman soldiers were there? Had the "creepy feelings" connected with Hulbert Road, Bedhampton any bearing on the tale of the man in the long mac seen by Joan and her son Steve (described in "Ghosts of Road and Rail"? [page 17].) Who can say?

49

Presentiments happen, and can be explained by coincidence or the reading of body language (as possibly happened in Mrs. Davis' presentiment that the child had died, in the first story in this section), but the following sad story is haunting in itself.

Peter Underwood tells of crew member Charlie Matthews' premonition that he would not return from an ill-fated voyage in the submarine L24 on manoeuvres in 1924. He told his wife, before he left Portsmouth to join his ship, that he had to go but would not return; that the boat would come up, go down again "and when we come up again we will be struck by something and that will be the end of us." Some days later, Mrs. Matthews heard her husband's voice call her name. She answered of course, but no one was there. At the same time a friend, staying at the house, thought she heard Mr. Matthews say: "Look after her ..."

By then, the L24 had sunk, in circumstances said to have been as those described by the sailor before his drowning.

The following, from an account by Ron Brown, also concerns the sinking of the L24.

Submariner Alfred Waterford's wife, Dolly, had a strong feeling that he would not return from the tour of duty which followed the Christmas home leave they had both enjoyed at Carter's Cottages, Forton Road, Gosport, in 1923. She saw him off and bade him goodbye in the January of 1924 from the tram stop, where she remained for some minutes, sure that something terrible would happen and that she would never again see the man she loved. One night shortly afterwards she awoke to hear his voice calling her name several times, then fading away... The following day Mrs. Waterford heard that her husband's submarine had sunk with all hands in a collision at sea off Portland, her 43 officers and men all lost.

Peter Underwood tells of a gardener at Craigie Lodge, Ventnor, who unearthed a child's jawbone while digging his employer's garden. He took it to the house, where Mrs. Pearl Craigie, his boss, was entertaining a friend, a Mrs. Hugh Pollock. The rest of the skeleton was dug out and Mrs. Pollock laid a bone from it against her forehead (an odd thing to do, but she was a psychometrist). She forecast that another skeleton would be found close to where the first one had been; a woman's skeleton was found as predicted, whether by coincidence, clairvoyance or deduction of probability is not stated.

The closet door came open

Michelle Petworth of Gosport, a hairdresser, stayed with a young friend whose mother owned the Redlands Inn, Fareham, in about 1989. She was told by the friend (a girl who has since emigrated with her family to Australia) that there was a ghost in her closet.

"We checked there was nothing in there before we went to bed," recalls Michelle - "but in the middle of the night, the closet door came open. I woke and saw a white figure - completely white - I don't know whether it was male or female...My head was right beside the closet door. I got into my friend's bed: I don't think I slept very well that night. It (the white figure) just went straight out of the bedroom and did not return. I never stayed there again."

Another time, she told me, as she styled my hair: "I don't know whether I believe in ghosts, but I know there's something else out there. I'm not afraid of things like that, since my Nan died: I know someone's watching over me."

(Many more strange experiences are described in "Spirited Inns and Haunted Pubs", p.27.)

Machine with an aura

Mrs. Horn of Meonstoke collects old sewing machines and bought one which she said gave out an aura.

"It seemed to say 'I must be used,' " she told me. "None of the others had this aura, only this one. It was a treadle."

It had been bought from a gentleman whose mother had used it to earn her living and, although it was dusty and dirty through disuse when Mrs. Horn bought it, when it was cleaned it was evident that it had been lovingly cared for by its previous lady owner.

"So I did eventually use it to make a quilt," she added, with a smile.

So does a ghostly seamstress rejoice to know her machine is loved and cared for again? We both hope so.

A Christchurch woman told me she had been confirmed into the Catholic church at 23 and before being accepted into the church went to weekly meetings with the priest. She told him she believed in "ghosts and spirits and things" and he told her that when he and his protege priest used to go into a particular church, "grey matter" would hover round the altar. It made him depressed. Then the younger priest saw it too. They looked around and found a little door with a skull and crossbones on it. They did an exorcism ... but the same thing happened in another church!

A flickering thing caught my eye

One afternoon, Mrs. Davis (see beginning of this "Strange Personal Experiences" section) saw something strange from the window of her home. It was "rather like a child's rubber swimming ring but silvery and spinning.

"I mean," she said, "I know what a plane looks like and it wasn't a plane. This flickering thing caught my eye; it moved from quite a bit above the ground on the left side of my window to further up on the right side. I bent down to see where it went as it rose but next door's chimney was in the way so I couldn't see it any more. I have never seen anything like it either before or since. It was going round as it moved, quite slowly ... but it glowed. It was so brief; I thought to myself: 'Don't be ridiculous, you must have imagined it,' but I don't think I did. I just do not know what it was. I have since read articles about flying saucers and things from outer space; in one I read that someone having a similar experience had contacted the army and they had said it was one of their weather devices the public didn't know about. I wonder if it was one of those ... or a balloon?"

She does not sound convinced.

HOUSE GUEST GHOSTS

There are a number of stories about ghosts which haunt houses large and small. Some are explained or partially explained with reference to historical events; others are totally inexplicable but represent real people's genuine experience, sincerely told.

Threw the only witness from an upstairs window ...

Alfred the Great mentioned Arreton Manor, Isle of Wight, in his will in AD 901. The monks of Quarr Abbey acquired land from Baldwin de Redvers in 1132 and, according to C.W.R. Winters, farmed the manor and lived in a house which preceded the present one on the site. When the abbey was closed at the Dissolution, Arreton had already been leased to John Leigh for 70 years. The lease passed to his son John, believed to be one of four brothers (Edward, Thomas, James and Barnaby). When John Leigh II and his wife Elizabeth died, Barnaby took over the lease. The story goes that in 1540, Thomas and James quarrelled over money. Their sword-fight on the stairs resulted in their deaths, from a punctured heart and other wounds, respectively. Barnaby is said to have been murdered in 1560 by his 13-year-old son John Leigh in order to inherit, after which Master Leigh threw his sister, the only witness, from an upstairs window to instant death. Gruesome!

The murders are considered unlikely, as the lad John grew up to be a Deputy Captain of the Island, a man of impeccable character unlikely to have done foul deeds; and the original number of brothers is historically hazy.

Little Annabelle, calling "Mama, mama!"

The present manor house was completed in 1612. There is ample scope for a ghost story in the above mixture of history and legend, so it is hardly surprising to read that there are sometimes sensed at Arreton an unexplained smell of incense and occasional chanting of monks. According to Underwood a monk or abbot in silver grey was seen near the Great Hall, associated with a whiff of incense, by Count Slade de Pomeroy and his housekeeper in 1980.

Sometimes, a woman in a red dress and the murdered child witness to the supposed murder are said to appear. They say little Annabelle, in blue dress and lacy slippers, has been seen walking through the house and garden, calling "Mama, mama!" Why she is called Annabelle when John Leigh's sister's name was Fortune is anybody's guess. You can't expect logic or historical accuracy from ghost stories. Winter suggests a connection with the once popular song about Annabelle Lee! It does not take much of a sideways thought leap to link the story with the song *My Sweet Little Alice Blue Gown*, but maybe I am allowing imagination to run riot.

Sword-play between bearded men with big hats ...

The house is open to the public. I was asked when I looked round if I felt a chill on the stairs. I did; I had left my sweater in the car. I heard in my mind the clatter of swords, saw dramatic sword-play between bearded men with big hats ... one of them was Errol Flynn, a hero of my teenage years. The scene was a flashback to a *Three Musketeers* movie; I think Flynn must have appeared in it to tell me how wonderful imagination can be. I left swiftly to search for sweater, sense and sunlight.

Did a sixteenth century sword-fight on the stairs really happen? And why do ghostly sword-fights so commonly occur on staircases? Hearsay can distort history. Many staff and visitors believe in the Annabelle legend and claim to have seen and heard the child. Underwood writes that it does not do to dismiss the story lightly.

A definite presence at the Wax Museum ...

Mr. Dave Cawte, business consultant and musician, of Swanmore, told my husband and I when we met him socially that he had "sensed something in the room at Arreton" and that he had also felt "a definite presence" at the Wax Museum, Brading, something "definitely not very nice", he told us. "We had a dog with us who was barking for no apparent reason. I had to leave in the end."

The Wax Museum, in an old house which was painted a garish pink when we visited, is reputedly haunted by Louis de Rochfort, a French nobleman who was murdered there and was by all accounts a far from pleasant person.

Disturbed when we put in double glazing ...

Mr. and Mrs. Martin Hall-Patch of Dibden Purlieu used to live in Bitterne Manor where Mr. Hall-Patch says there was a mischievous spirit, probably that of a former owner, a shipwright, who had made all the woodwork.

"We only disturbed him (the spirit) when we put in the double glazing," he said; "we called him Fred, although that was not his real name, and told him to behave himself. We thought he resented our altering his handiwork. You'd see something move on the mantlepiece and say: 'Stop it, Fred.' He only once did anything really malevolent - my wife was scared - things were thrown at her in the kitchen when I was out; not just moved - thrown! It was a mess; things were broken."

Indelible bloodstains ...

Bordean House at Langrish, now a Sue Ryder Home, was built in 1611 as a private house, became a rest centre for Royal Naval personnel in the 2nd World War, then a home to nuns. It is said to have three ghosts: a cavalier who wears his hat and cloak in the house (how ungallant!); a white lady who walks the drive then vanishes; and a ghost connected with a duel in which one of two adversarial brothers died. Proof of the latter incident is claimed to be an indelible blood stain on the chapel floor. Indelible bloodstains occur in folk tales: remember Bluebeard?

They all thought the others would think they were stupid ...

Mr. Dan Davies of Bognor Regis tells the story of a ghost near Segensworth at Lee Ground, in the civil parish of Wickham, eastwards of the M27 and to its northern side. There are dwellings marked on a 1960's O.S. map with plots marked in long thin strips.

"It was at the back of Knowle Hospital near the Segensworth roundabout, land now close to the M27. On it there was a collection of large bungalows in one of which my mother lived as a child. The bungalow stood on six acres of ground with a smallholding and she lived there with her sister, mother and stepfather.

"The bedrooms of the bungalow were in a line, although not connected, and this is important to the story. Well, members of the family used to see a figure walk through the bedrooms, in through one wall and out through another, and no one said anything because they all thought the others would think they were stupid or something. Then eventually one of them must have mentioned what they'd seen - a man in a shabby brown coat - and they realised they had all seen the same thing. Local folklore was that the bungalow was built on the site of an old coaching inn. They tried to get it exorcised (they were a Catholic family). I don't know what happened after that.

"It happened after the First World War, for my father was there then. He worked in Portsmouth Dockyard; cycled to and from work every day from Segensworth and worked the smallholding in his spare time. They worked so hard in those days. He died while they lived there. My grandmother had remarried and my mother was a teenager of about 14 to 18 by the time the family saw the ghost; it must have happened in, say, 1925 or 1926."

There is no record of a coaching house on those maps I have consulted, but there may be one on a much older map.

Reports appeared in the national press in 1967 of a "haunted cottage" in Ringwood , believed to date from the early eighteenth century, where a Georgian couple were seen by the children of the house and their friends. The 'ghosts' were invisible to adults. It is known that children can hear the shrill cries of bats more readily than adults; some say they can also sense the supernatural more readily than older people do. (See also "Churches and Churchyards" chapter, p.89)

The lady in the portrait looked grim ...

Breamore House is the home of Mr. Edward Hulse, whose family has owned it for generations. The Doddingtons built the house in 1583; James I knighted a William Doddington 20 years later and William's wife was murdered by their son Henry, for which deed

Henry was hanged at Winchester Gaol in 1630. The first Lady Doddington is said to haunt the Blue Bedroom where reputedly the murder took place.

Breamore House is now open to the public. The first Lady Doddington has not been seen for some time; this is just as well, for when she appears the owner of the house, it is said, will die. To touch her picture, known as the "accursed portrait", is also supposed to be lethal. When we visited, our guide told us no one had had the nerve to move it during the 2nd World War, when other household treasures were packed away and the services took over for the duration. The lady in the portrait looked grim ... I wonder how they do the dusting?

Which they took to be the coachman, returned to the scene of his crime ...

Testwood House, Totton, has a facade which hides an older building formerly used as a hunting lodge by Edward VI and Henry VIII when they stayed in the New Forest. It became a private house in which either a butler and a coachman fought for the favours of the lady's maid, or the dastardly butler, to end an affair of which he had tired, murdered the cook and dumped the body at the start of what is now Cook's Lane, or both - take your pick. The building became a bonded warehouse for sherry. Loud noises were heard in its attic towards the end of the nineteenth century and more recently staff and children experienced lights going off by themselves, or saw a cloaked figure silhouetted in the hall, which they took to be the coachman, returned to the scene of his crime. A formerly mild-mannered guard dog refused to go into the room where the murder is believed to have taken place.

It would be nice to know more about the lady with the candle ...

At a farm in Wickham, two brothers, on their own and on different occasions, slept in the same room. Each said they had seen there a woman in a long white robe, carrying a candle, but neither mentioned her at the time. My informant's former boyfriend was another of the brothers.

"It was a very cold room," said the girl; "it was a very cold farm. Very run down. We were in a pub, when one brother described what he had seen and the other brother said 'I saw her too'; but they might have been winding me up, knowing that I was susceptible to that kind of thing. I don't know."

This storyteller does not wish to be named. If the brothers' stories were a hoax, it shows how some ghost stories may originate. If it were true, it would be nice to know more about the lady with the candle. Is there anyone out there who can tell me more?

I wonder what he made of the vacuum cleaner?

Jill Forman (1978) and Jill Belcher in The *News* write of Mrs. Rosemary Stevens, whose house was built about 1950 in Waterlooville on a once wooded site; trees at the end of the garden merged with the wood at the end of the plot and a stile from the old woodland path led from the garden into the wood.

One sunny midday, workmen were cutting oak trees in the wood prior to a new road being built; Mrs. Stevens, busy hoovering her dining room, felt she was being watched, turned off her machine and through the open french window saw a grey figure which stood on the old pathway, in the garden, dressed in "something like a ploughman's smock" and hat. There was a "sad emanation". Mrs. Stevens took the event calmly, even when the figure vanished. She told no one about it except her family, until her butcher, a local man, called at the house. She asked him whether there had been a tragedy in the area.

The butcher told her his father's tale of a century earlier: a cattle drover used to drive herds to market from Hambledon down the track which was part of the Stevens's garden. One market-day the man's cattle strayed; local people knew how careful the drover usually was of his stock and looked for him. The searchers found the drover's body hanging from a large oak near where the Stevens's house now stood.

Mrs. Stevens told the butcher of her ghostly experience. He suggested the developers may have destroyed the oak, so precipitating a haunting. Ms. Forman suggests this is not unreasonable, on the grounds that interference with material surroundings can not only end a haunting but bring one into being, and that the imprint of the sad old man may have been transmitted by a tree. Mrs. Stevens saw his sad shape several times; it became fainter and disappeared each time she tried to talk to it. Although she pointed it out several times, members of her family were unable to see it or to feel its sadness.

If ghosts there be, perhaps this lady's calm acceptance of her strange visitor and her attempts to offer comforting words released him, poor soul. I wonder what he made of the vacuum cleaner?

A lady in blue haunts Palace House, Beaulieu [See page 61]

Morganatic wife ...

Redrice School near Stockbridge is a house once owned by George IV. Mrs. Fitzherbert, his morganatic wife when he was Prince of Wales, is said to haunt it occasionally.

A ghost in one of their previous houses ...

Mrs. M. Wood of Westleigh, Havant, lives with her husband, a retired quality control inspector, in a house built in 1957 which they moved into when it was new. Mrs. Wood believes strongly in ghosts and at one time had an interest in spiritualism.

"At a time of considerable strain" she told me, "I used to see a man at the bottom of the stairs. He was not very clear - he looked kind of beige and I couldn't see his face. I used to think he was an Indian or something. Whenever I saw him, I'd say: 'Hello? You again!' I used to walk through him, you see. There was no fear. I wish I knew why these things happen."

As a child of between seven and ten, in about 1933-1936, when she lived with her parents in Stamshaw, Portsmouth, she says she would wake in the night to see her pillow "glowing gold, as if there were electric lights inside the pillow". She adds: "It was very comforting, actually. I never told anyone about it, until now. I just used to sit back and watch until the colour faded." This happened in an old house, "a tiny terraced house", built, she thinks, about 1898.

Her parents, she added, had a ghost in one of their previous houses in the same area; they used to hear footsteps in a first-floor room when they were downstairs, always accompanied by the sound of the blind going up, when there was really no one there. This observer's calm acceptance of her strange visitor is similar to that of Mrs. Stevens.

Slump in the housing market ...

Mr. Steve West of New Milton near Christchurch told me in 1995:

"There is a lovely cottage on Bashley crossroads - a picture-postcard cottage with white walls and a thatched roof - I have always admired it. A 'for sale' sign was up every time I passed it, over a period of perhaps three years, but because of the slump in the housing market and the difficulties I knew people were having over negative equity,

60

I thought no more about it.

"I work in a bank. One day a colleague who was dealing with the property on the market told me the reason for it not having been sold: it was haunted. In the past at some point there had been a murder or sudden death in this property involving a couple. In two years, two couples had successively bought the property and each of their marriages had broken up within less than a year. Each couple cited the very unhappy atmosphere in the cottage as contributory to their own unhappiness in it, and each maintained that their marriage had previously been happy. A third couple consulted my colleague to ask him to arrange a mortgage and had told him this story. So far, couple number three appeared to be okay."

I do hope so. Perhaps the jinx or whatever it was has worn off. Or were the previous marriage break-ups coincidental?

Literary ghosts

Edmund Spenser, the Elizabethan poet who wrote *The Faerie Queen*, is said to return from time to time, in period costume, to his former home in Amery Street, Alton. Alfred Lord Tennyson's home at Farringdon, near Freshwater, Isle of Wight, has been converted into a hotel; visitors on request may see his library. The poet's ghost, in the distinctive wide-brimmed hat he used to wear (and which was a source of amusement to the locals), is said to appear from time to time on the walks he used to take from the house and around Freshwater.

Lady in blue

Palace House, Beaulieu, was once the gatehouse of the abbey. Now the home of Lord Montagu, it is said to be haunted by a number of ghosts, one of whom is supposed to be Isabella, wife of the 2nd Duke. She is known as the Lady in Blue.

A ghostly Quaker has been said to appear at Bramshott Court, especially when it was used as a First World War army hospital. *Friendly phantoms ...*

Hermitage, a house in Gosport, is believed locally to have been built on a monastery site and to have been haunted by friendly phantoms. Three Dutch Catholic brothers and their sister, refugees from religious persecution, lived there in about 1730.

Noise of a fight and the scent of lilies ...

Billingham Manor on the Isle of Wight is said by some to be the most haunted house on the island, but this may be a consequence of it having been rented at one time by Sir Shane Leslie, a famous ghost-hunter. Reported incidents range from things which bumped loudly in the night via the disembodied head of Charles I, to the scent of Madonna Lilies. Stories include those of four people who committed some sin and remained attached to the house after death; Winter was told by medium Mrs. Margo Williams that she had contacted and released three of them, all members of the Worsley family. Some historians agree (but others don't) that the Worsleys lived at the house at the time the events in the stories are supposed to have taken place.

Peter Underwood was told by Sir Shane Leslie in 1960 that when he and his wife lived at Billingham he saw the severed royal head. Charles I is said to have hidden behind a sliding panel in the drawing room at the manor, after his escape from imprisonment at Carisbrook Castle. The accommodation was so cramped he returned to captivity rather than remain there. Sir Shane and his lady discovered a refuge where the King might have hidden, after they had been disturbed at night by footfalls and sword-clanks. One night, the noises became really violent, the whole household was awakened and trooped to the drawing room, where they all saw the king's head glow and disappear.

That's the story - and there's more. A prisoner was executed at Newport the very same day in 1928 that they saw the apparition. Also, Sir Shane had found a diary of a former owner in which it was written that each time he had seen an identical apparition of King Charles' severed head, an Island execution had taken place!

Another tale concerns Jane Leigh of Idlecombe, who was in love with a young Frenchman and therefore unwilling to marry Edward Worsley in 1708. He married her all the same; women did not have much choice in those days. When Edward caught his young wife with her lover the two men fought with swords on the stairs into the garden, Jane hurled a scent bottle at her husband and piteously pleaded with him to spare the young man's life. Nevertheless, he killed him, in the circumstances probably the only acceptable action he could have taken, according to male manners of the time, but Jane's situation does not bear thinking about. Worsley punished her by confining her to the morning-room, allowed out only to do her wifely duty of giving orders to the cook. She remained bound to the house, it is said, from her death in 1741 until reputedly freed by Mrs. Williams in July 1978, after which the noise of the fight and the scent of lilies were no longer experienced.

Various residents at Billingham have reported seeing a "grey lady", supposedly Jane Worsley. Visitors said they saw her when there was no actual woman in the house. A Canadian General billeted at Billingham during the 2nd World War was scared by noises at night. The present owners are not reported to have seen or heard anything unusual.

I mentioned the King Charles story in a broadcast on Radio Solent with Sandy Jones. She asked how it was that Charles I lost his head in London but it came back to haunt Billingham. There was no answer to that.

That one bride should be lost in this way is unfortunate ...

Bramshill Police Staff College is at seventeenth century Bramshill House which was sold to the Home Office in 1953. It is on the site of a manor house which was present long before the Domesday Book and is reputed to have as nice a collection of ghosts - at least eleven if you don't count the ghostly group which floats in the chapel drawing room - as I have heard of anywhere in Hampshire. One is a gamekeeper, who was carelessly shot with a crossbow in 1621 by a deer-hunting Archbishop of Canterbury, a guest of Lord Zouche (who demolished the previous building to put up the present one). Another is the bride who allegedly hid in the Mistletoe Bough Chest (now in the hall of the college) during a game of hide-and-seek at her Christmas wedding celebrations, where she remained until a housekeeper found her corpse 50 years later. (Children this century have been trapped inside abandoned fridges or freezers in much the same way; such things were not designed to be opened from within.)

Anyhow, the Bramshill bride is supposed to be the sad-faced lady in white, sightings of whom have been reported over the years. Her perfume heralds her appearance. The same story is told of Marwell House and is heard in Europe too. That one bride should be lost in this way is unfortunate; that another Hampshire bride should be similarly mislaid is peculiar; but that the same unlikely set of circumstances should occur in Europe too, reputedly more than once, verges on the ridiculous. I wonder where it began?

Green man with no legs ...

Sir John Cope became the owner of Bramshill in 1699; his family held it for almost two and a half centuries. One of the Cope children, when very young, reported seeing, near water, a green man with no legs. Her parents thought, reasonably enough, that this was a childish fantasy. But her eccentric ancestor, Henry Cope, was known to have had a strong preference for the colour green (had he lived, would he have joined the Green Party?). He ate only greens, dressed in green, furnished green rooms with green furniture and travelled in a green gig, became insane in 1806 (surprise!) and died by falling over the cliffs at Brighton. He has been linked with the Cope child's fantasy, which, if you remember, had no legs. This has been explained. Henry Cope could not get green boots, so wore black ones. So? Well, that's the end of that story.

The Bramshill apparitions surprise - sometimes amuse - people, rather than frighten them. Except, that is, for the drowned gardener near the lake who scares people and dogs. Bramshill is a ghost-hunter's paradise, but is usually full of policemen.

At Bramshott, it is said that a white lady haunts the manor and that a drowned Mistress Butler walks beside the water. Unlike the gardener in the previous story, she does not scare anyone.

The old lady of the house ...

A former manager of a Hampshire electronics firm recently went with his friend to visit at an old house at Compton. Their hosts took them for a drink at their local pub, but as my informant and his friend preferred to drink coffee, it was suggested they make their way back to the house towards the end of the evening and start to brew up. Their hosts promised to be back shortly.

In their hosts' kitchen, the couple started to set out cups and coffee-making equipment. My informant had his back towards his friend, when he felt the hair on the back of his neck stand on end. He turned to find her transfixed and looking at something he could not see, which she followed with her eyes towards a wall.

"Keep still, it's the old lady of the house," she said. As she relaxed, my informant said:

"She's gone, hasn't she?"

"Yes," said his friend. "She's gone out of the door."

"But there isn't a door there!" the man exclaimed.

"Well, there used to be," his friend assured him.

"I was a disbeliever" (in the supernatural), my informant went on, "until this happened. My friend believed she had seen a ghost and although I had not seen it, I had felt its chill and an uncanny feeling, though I had not even been looking in her direction. I think some people are more susceptible to this sort of thing than others. She sensed a chill in another house we visited, built about the 1920's, in which a child had died in rather peculiar circumstances."

Something white was floating down the hall ...

After hearing my broadcast, Mrs. Eunice Longhurst of Southbourne, Bournemouth, sent me the following account of a ghostly happening:

"About thirty years ago I was living with my family in an old house in Southampton. I had two young children and no central heating, so the children dressed and undressed in front of the living-room fire.

"After a busy day spring cleaning, washing nets, re-hanging etc., I rushed upstairs to collect the children's pyjamas from their beds. It was cold and the hall badly lit; I shot into the bedroom, grabbed the pyjamas and as I trotted back along the top hall, something caught my eye. Horror! Something white was floating behind me down the hall! I ran: it followed! With a shriek I dropped the pyjamas and leapt the stairs, not seeming to touch as I came down, screaming hysterically as I went. Everyone rushed out of the living-room and after a few minutes, when I had calmed down and stopped screaming, I gasped 'GHOST!' and pointed upstairs. My brave husband rushed upstairs, could find nothing, but returned carrying the abandoned pyjamas, attached to which by a button was a net curtain . As he carried the pyjamas downstairs, it followed behind, floating realistically ghost-like behind him. We ended up in fits of laughter and I never lived it down!"

Does the grey shape of Lady Jane Worsley still flit from room to room in the house where her husband confined her? [See page 63]

SMUGGLING CONNECTIONS

A nod and a wink or a coded message ...

The Hampshire coast was ideal for landing goods from the big contraband warehouses across the Channel in the Golden Age of smuggling, before 1815. Prevailing south-westerly winds brought fast sailing ships to sandy beaches where goods were unloaded and hidden, prior to being carried down quiet tracks and paths to market in inland cities and towns. The Revenue service was poorly staffed and financed. Hampshire smugglers had a relatively easy time for many years, often with the collusion of local gentry, townsfolk and villagers, whose attitude was so delightfully portrayed by Rudyard Kipling in his *Smuggler's Song*, which advises a child not to look out into the street if she wakes at midnight, for:

> Them that asks no questions isn't told a lie;
> Watch the wall my darling while the Gentlemen go by.

Smuggled tea, brandy and silks could be obtained much more cheaply than they could be bought legally. Secrecy was essential during the unloading of contraband on local shores; the rendezvous would be arranged as late as possible, at different suitable drop-points, at different times, word of which would be passed on to the smugglers as they went about their normal business by a nod and a wink or a coded message. Morley writes of a milkmaid who carried yoked buckets around the streets of Christchurch; the number of floats on each bucket respectively indicated to the smugglers the date and time of the next landing.

When the Napoleonic Wars ended, smugglers had a difficult time, as the navy was available to search any ship suspected of carrying illegal cargo. Rumours of hauntings are known to have been used in a number of places to keep the inquisitive away. I suspect any story close to a smuggling route may have been fabricated or at least encouraged, in order to help smugglers and their accomplices to escape detection.

A whistling ghost ...

At Warblington, Lady Margaret, Countess of Salisbury, is said to drift headless along the lane from Warblington church, through the churchyard and across fields. The sixteenth century castle she lived in was later destroyed by the Roundheads in the English Civil War. She lost her head at the Tower of London for opposing Henry VIII at the Reformation. This is why, I suppose, she does not have it with her - although Lady Alicia Lisle managed to retain hers, albeit to wear underneath her arm, having been similarly decapitated. A ghostly smuggler killed in a quarrel is also said to haunt Warblington Castle; and Pook Lane, Havant, the start of a direct route northwards which was used to distribute contraband goods, was once known as Spook Lane and said to have a whistling ghost - as convenient a cover for smugglers' signals as I ever heard told...

Frank Westwood's *Account of Hayling Island* tells of a smuggler, Ralph, who was coming back from a trip when his wife or girl-friend, Jane Rogers, learned the Revenue men were close by. She set off to warn him, was mistaken by Ralph for a pursuer and shot. A similar story is told about a ghostly figure said to cross the road "level with Warblington Castle" onto the mud-flats. A Havant man told me he knows someone who claims to have seen this figure "but it might just have been the effect of swirling mist". He wonders how the ghost manages, now the new stretch of dual carriageway (A27 bypass) takes traffic across the old smuggling route. I was not given the source of his information; ghost stories often happen to a friend of a friend.

He did not know whether the ghost was male or female ...

Langstone Mill, the Royal Oak and the Ship Inn at Langstone were smugglers' haunts; the mill tower was an ideal spot from which members of the Langstone Gang could signal to those at sea waiting to bring in contraband goods and from which, after the Coastguard was formed, to observe the activities of Coastguard vessels. These were often moored in the harbour so that the Revenue men could look out for the smugglers who were looking out for them, in a constant deadly game of cat-and-mouse!

The Royal Oak in Langstone High Street was probably built in the mid-sixteenth century and was at one time a bakery which supplied Nelson's fleet with fresh bread. It is known to have been licensed since 1727 and is a popular eating place, especially in summer. It stands beside the harbour, the tide comes right up to the front door, and the pub is reputed to be haunted.

After publicity about possible hauntings, a correspondent wrote to a local newspaper to say that he was born at 20 Langstone (later named the High Street) in a house attached to the Royal Oak. His father held the inn licence in 1905 and his grandmother and some relatives lived in the inn. "There was no ghost there when I was there," he wrote "nor did I hear anyone in the village mention one."

However, the wife of a former landlord is reported to have awoken one night to feel someone was in her bedroom. Believing it to be her daughter, she sat up to see a tall female figure glide slowly from the room. Meanwhile, her daughter remained asleep in her own bed. Unexplained footsteps and noises were heard, "like chains being moved on the floor of the empty public bar". Her spaniel howled, trembled, and bristled when left to sleep there and would never again remain in the bar.

I asked the 1995 landlord, Mr. Stuart Warren, if he had any evidence that the pub was haunted. He said that he and his wife had only been at the Royal Oak six months but that they had "heard some noises; it sounded like furniture moving about". Locals had said, "Oh, yes, there were a couple of dogs years ago who would not go in the bar." Mrs. Joan Spring and her husband, previous licensees, had dashed out of their room at night with a torch when footsteps reached the top of the stairs but there was no one there!

"We've come downstairs and found the bar stool moved - things like that," Mr. Warren told me. "It's all part of the fun of being here;

that and the floods we get at high tides. There was an article about it in the local newspaper and a lot of tourists take photographs; they love it."

He did not know whether the ghost was male or female, he said, but there was supposed to be an undiscovered passage to the mill (a passage is believed to have connected smugglers' hides at the mill, the Royal Oak and the Ship) and that in the short time they had been at the Royal Oak, he and his wife had been disturbed about four times. He had been downstairs to check what was happening.

"It's always exceptionally cold and pitch black, except for moonlight through the windows - you know how warm you feel when you've just got out of bed? - and you have to walk through the restaurant to get to the lights. With a dressing-gown and slippers on, it's still really cold. We've seen no one, though. I go back to bed and my wife's still hiding under the duvet. The first time we heard the noises, 'Oh, bloody hell,' I said, and hid under the duvet too - you know? Any excuse for a cuddle, and the building's alarmed anyhow ... Two of my staff have refused our offer to stay overnight, though; they say 'thanks, we'd like to, but no thanks!' "

It is only fair to add that, whereas the ghostly smuggler stories are romantic and lend themselves to amusing illustration, Lady Margaret features in one explanation of the haunting at the Royal Oak and a priest who hid in a priest's hole behind a panel in the bathroom features in another. Maybe there are several ghosts (the more the merrier, especially in licensed premises!).

To meet his lady by the old burial ground ...

A Napoleonic French naval officer who died imprisoned in a hulk offshore would return, it's said, to meet his lady by the old Gosport burial ground. Was this ghostly tale encouraged to deter the Revenue men? He has not been seen since recent building development.

Rolled brandy barrels

At Pylewell Home Farm, east of where the Lymington River meets the sea, it is claimed that the sound of brandy barrels can be heard as they are rolled across upper floors by ghostly Lymington smugglers who in life used the farm as a smuggling dump.

Eerie cries and monkish plainsong ...

Geoffrey Morley says there is a tradition that Beaulieu Abbey ruins were used as a brandy depot for goods brought in via the Beaulieu River; there, fine cognac was made "fit for English tastes"; also, Palace House, Beaulieu was probably used as a smugglers' look-out point (a staircase goes through the house to a secret chapel beneath the roof). The smugglers would terrify anyone who came too near the abbey, including the occasional residents of Palace House, by uttering "eerie cries and monkish plainsong".

A small, flickering light ...

Mr. D.J. Stevenson of Stafford Road, Petersfield, writes of an incident when he was on holiday with his parents in about 1937, staying with an aunt in Finchdean Road, Rowland's Castle.

"One evening, we all went to Portsmouth for a club outing on a paddle steamer. For some reason, the boat was very late getting us back to dry land and as a result we could only get a train as far as Havant. We'd have to walk the rest!

"I vaguely remember the long, stumbling walk from Havant along a quiet lane, now a dual carriageway ..." (this must be the Petersfield Road through Leigh Park) "... in pitch darkness. We walked through the village - all the houses in darkness as it was now the early hours of the morning - and under the arches into Finchdean Road. The only gas lamp, at the beginning of the road, was not on. The huge beech trees in Stansted Park made the blackness more intense than ever. We all held onto each other and literally had to feel our way along.

We hadn't gone far when a small, flickering light *suddenly* appeared in front of us, seemingly about 20 yards ahead. It appeared to be a candle in an old-fashioned lantern. I say it appeared suddenly; there was no impression that anyone had come onto the path from an opening and I saw no sign that anyone had struck a match or lit it in any way. It just appeared. As we stumbled on, it started to move too, in the same direction as us. It was swinging as it would do if being carried by a handle at the top. I could hear no footsteps and the loom of the light didn't seem to cast any light on the carrier's legs or feet. It acted as a good leading light and kept on, the same distance ahead of us all along the road, until we reached our front gate. As we did so, it disappeared as suddenly as it had appeared. The adults called out to say 'thanks!' but there was no reply.

"Naturally my parents, aunt and uncle talked about it in the village over the next few days; my father used the local pub and talked to several of the very old villagers that he knew. These old folk didn't seem at all surprised. 'Why, it's just the smugglers!' they said. It turned out that a few of them had seen a similar light at some time or other and many more knew about it. Finchdean Road apparently was part of the old smugglers' route from Langstone harbour to Rake and on northwards, and local folk lore had it that what we had seen was the ghost of one of them, leading the way along the road.

"All this happened to me a long time ago, but it was so strange that it is something that I have never been able to forget. I can see that light as clearly as if it had just happened. It *could* have been a hoax, but if it was it was a very clever one. I am not a believer in ghosts, either, but I've never been able to come up with any other explanation. None of our family ever saw the light again."

He smiled and left, leaving the door open.

Both Underwood and Winter write of the wife of a former landlord at the White Hart at Basingstoke who heard the sound of something being rolled over gravel, sometimes so loudly it prevented her sleeping, always after midnight. A number of different people at different times are said to have heard the same sounds (barrels being rolled by phantom smugglers?) and the licensee's mother was reported to have seen a man in the 'haunted' room who smoothed back his hair, smiled and left, leaving the door open.

Brandy barrels are heard trundling by Adams Cottage, Bramshott, "when there is a smugglers' moon", according to Ian Fox.

At Burley, the apparition of a weeping, small boy is said to have been seen running along an old smugglers' track to Picket Post, in the New Forest. It disappears among rushes in marshy ground; also, nearer the coast, where the Lymington-Milford road crosses a stream, a small headless boy ghost, so they say, would sit on the parapet of Cox's Bridge. These sightings have been linked with the macabre story of a couple who lived near an old claypit or brickyard near Burley; at an unspecified time, long ago, they are reputed to have drowned at least one of their children in a nearby pool because they could not afford to feed them.(Yuk! Is this another version of the "Babes in the Wood" tale which used to frighten me so much as a child?). It is significant that the ghost was seen on a smugglers' path, so maybe the story was invented to keep away prying eyes. I hope it was ...

Ghost stories at Netley Abbey may have been similarly encouraged. There was storage space in the abbey vaults and the castle, no longer garrisoned by 1627, could have been used, Geoffrey Morley suggests, as a smugglers' watch point and signalling station. As a gentleman's residence, it had fine possibilities as point of sale for smuggled goods brought in from Southampton Water. Indeed, it may well be that the area's smuggler chief, Russel, was the 'gentleman' who lived at Netley Castle, as its ownership is mysterious until more recent times. Russel is recorded as having lured the Preventative Officer (of the Board of Customs) away from a favourite 'drop' for smuggled goods, by loading a decoy lugger with what looked like brandy kegs but what turned out to be straw replicas.

The Cottage Bar at Abbots's Ann was a derelict 500-year-old inn, bought in the early 1960's and renovated by Charles Bowyer. Unexplained activity reported during the renovations and said to be ghostly was connected locally with stories of a London lady responsible for wild "goings on" in the eighteenth century. Later, footsteps were heard in the building, doors slammed and a vague, possibly female, form was seen near the stairs when no one was supposed to be there. There is also said to be a tunnel, of unknown purpose, leading from the cellar to the river. Did a reckless lady ghost, squatters or smugglers invade the premises from time to time? What a wild party if they all turned up at once to dispose of the smuggled brandy!

The Hayling Island Wild Cat, now in the safe custody of Portsmouth Museums [see page 80]

A ghostly donkey that is said to inhabit Damerham [see page 7⁹]

DOGS, CATS AND OTHER ASSORTED ANIMALS

It is said that animals are especially receptive to the supernatural. *Folklore, Myths and Legends of Britain* records that to dogs and horses are commonly ascribed the power to see ghosts. When they do, horses shy and sweat and dogs snarl, although the spirits are invisible to humans. Horse brasses were used at least until the 1940's to protect horses from the evil eye, in traditional spirit-repelling shapes such as the sun and the crescent moon. Cats are supposed to be fond of ghosts so they purr when they encounter one. There is controversy about the nature of alien big cats which have been reported from time to time.

Dogs are mentioned in a house-ghost story at Totton and Hayling, in pub ghost stories at Langstone and Upham and in the following one at Alton.

Black dog in an Alton Hotel

At Alton a phantom dog was reputedly heard for many years at the Crown Hotel. It whimpered and scratched. It was said to be the spirit of an animal flung against a chimney breast by its drunken master. One landlady's two dogs became agitated when they approached the fireplace; behind it, in 1967, workmen discovered the skeleton of a dog but the two stories may be connected solely by place. The 'hauntings' went on after the canine skeleton was removed. Inexplicable paw marks were found on the bar in 1985; a resident barman is said to have met a phantom black dog (he thought it was the landlord's dog) in the dining-room. However, the landlord's pet was behind the bar at the time. On being told the hotel's ghost story, the man left and would not come back - a pity, for the apparition seemed harmless enough. This story is interesting in that the barman saw the supposedly phantom dog, not knowing that the Crown was reputed to be haunted. It is also interesting because phantom black hounds are recorded in folk stories throughout England. They are maybe related to tales of the Wild Hunt which led the Norse god, Woden, by moonlight, the sight of which was fatal to mortals. Not surprisingly, black dog stories occur mostly in northern England and in the Midlands and were possibly imported with the Vikings.

The only further "black dog" story I have found in Hampshire refers to the ghostly black dog which at one time is said to have haunted the area around Abbot's Ann, near Andover. A farm worker who, they say, met it twice, was alarmed when he swiped at it with a stick which when straight through the beastie.

A half-gravestone was dug up ...

A Staffordshire bull terrier which came with visitors to a seventeenth century Droxford cottage was one of those who heard footsteps. The dog hid under a settee and would not come out until the noise had stopped. Bumps and footsteps had already been heard in the room above by the people who lived there, usually as they sat downstairs in the evening but in daytime too, when no one was there. Later, their garden wall had to be replaced and a half-gravestone was dug up on which was half a memorial inscription to a husband and wife. The name on the stone tallied with an entry in the parish register recording the death in 1679 of Beatrice Hatch. The gravestone was linked with the strange noises, one of those tenuous links with which unusual happenings are attached to historical events to produce a ghost story. The occupants of the house were comfortable with their 'ghost'; only the dog was alarmed.

New Forest ponies are said to shy away from Hazeley Copse, an area near Godshill, Fordingbridge, where local legend says there was a "Roman Massacre".

This inefficient villain accidentally hanged himself ...

A much documented story is that of Mrs. Forse, one time rector's wife at Rowland's Castle, who used to walk her dog in the woods near the old rectory. A local nineteenth century poacher, or highwayman-robber, Charlie Pearce, is said to haunt Gypsy's Clump nearby. This inefficient villain accidentally hanged himself by catching his neck in the branch of a tree when drunk. Mrs. Forse was looking for ivy for Christmas church decorations, according to Brode, when she saw a horse and rider. The rider wore a fawn cloak or coat in accounts by three different writers. She glanced away and - he was gone; nothing was left but thick vegetation either side of where she had thought him to be. Her dog rushed home ahead of her and was found shaking.

A former schoolteacher in the village, Miss Daisy Baker, claimed to have seen Charlie's ghost frequently. Sometimes it was riding down the St. John's church pathway, only to vanish at the school where she taught for 50 years. Rowland's Castle new rectory is nowhere near the woods. An elderly gentleman member of the church congregation, who has lived in the village for some years, told me in February 1995 that he had "never heard anyone in the village complain of ghosts" and pointed out that the church, built in 1837, post-dates the days of highwaymen. I could not find anyone in Rowland's Castle who had met a phantom horseman on the church path, nor any other phantom in Rowland's Castle either, until I heard from Mr. Weatherby of Halfpenny Lane, Old Portsmouth.

Her growling was getting louder and louder ...

Mr. Weatherby writes that in the Spring of 1977, the first really light evenings, he was contacted to refurbish three old cottages that were end-on to the Green, alongside the Robin Hood pub, Rowland's Castle. At that time, he had a Pyranean Mountain dog, called Reona; she always accompanied him to work, being quite happy to lie down and sleep, wherever he might be busy. He was upstairs in the cottage nearest to the Green, fixing the built-in wardrobes, when footsteps trotted across the boarded-out roof space above his head. He thought it was the tilers, come back to finish off the ridge tiles, so ignored the sounds. The footsteps continued, back and forth. Then he heard his dog growling, very softly.

"Now, Reona had been asleep in the downstairs hallway," he

77

continues; "but when I walked onto the landing, she was standing, looking up at the open trap-hatch. Her lips were drawn right back and all the hair on her body was standing out straight. Her growling was getting louder and louder and she was beginning to snarl.

"I fetched my short ladder and climbed to the roof. I switched on the light; ... nothing! The roof was empty.

"Now, originally, the roof space had run from one end of the building to the other but I had built fire-protection walls, to separate the cottages' long roof space into units. As I stood there, the footsteps trotted past me, going towards the back of the building. Within a couple of minutes they returned; then they did the same thing, all over again. I realised that on their return trip, they trotted slower. They had to be carrying something. They were loading something out. I left them to get on with it. I grabbed the dog by the collar and put her in the van, out of harm's way, then locked up and went home.

"I found out from one of the old men that drank in the pub that years before, when he had been a youngster, a man loading out and taking sacks of grain off a pulley hoist at the end of the building had slipped and fallen out of the door, onto the cobbled yard, and been killed. I think the work on the old cottages disturbed the ghost."

Mr. Weatherby seems to have taken this experience very calmly, being concerned only for his dog.

The dogs would move aside ...

A man in black was said to haunt the fifteenth century Old Fleet Manor House at Hayling Island, occupied by Colonel Sheppard in 1943-1960. Built near the site of a former priory, the house may have contained part of the original priory building work. The Colonel's dogs would move aside as if to allow an invisible person to pass; one dog jumped out of the window rather than stay in a room in which its owner thought it saw something which he couldn't see. The Colonel once felt someone gently stroke his head. He interpreted the stroking as a blessing and thought the man in black must have been the spectre of a priest. He was not alarmed by the supposed ghost (he neither moved aside nor jumped out of the window) but after Colonel Sheppard sold the house, the new owner's domestic help saw the man in black and left.

Two hollow eyes and no legs ...

Mrs. W. Lemonton of Woolston, Southampton, had a dog which she said saw a ghost in 1966 at the same time as she did, one afternoon in her hallway. The dog ran to it and barked. She described the apparition as a thing with two hollow eyes and no legs, which approached her, stood on the bottom stair then went through the lounge wall. Although it scared her a bit at the time it did no harm. Whew!

A sort of sixth sense ...

Mrs. Horn of Meonstoke told us of a place on the disused Meon Valley railway line where "even horses, now, going along, won't go". 24 years earlier she had been told there had been some sort of accident there on the railway.

"I mean, you can be quite logical and say ghosts don't exist, but animals have a sort of sixth sense, haven't they?"

Dogs growled ...

Dogs have growled and showed signs of unease when passing a yew tree, beneath which money was reputedly hidden by a wealthy woman who lived at nearby Windmill Cottage, Braishfield.

A black pig and a ghostly white donkey ...

A black pig has been said to appear and disappear in fields at Bramshott near the church. A ghostly donkey is said to walk through the village of Damerham, to vanish in the old sawpit.

A fairy calf ...

A white fairy calf, so they say, trots along lanes near Liphook and jumps hedges. Sometimes it shrinks in size (like Alice); or alternatively, vanishes. It has links with the mysterious boy ghost described on page 20.

The *Fortean Times* lists sightings of cat-like creatures, termed 'alien big cats' or ABCs, in many places in Britain, usually large and black; although glimpses of such creatures have been seen from time to time, it is rare for any pictures but long range or shadowy ones to be obtained and only very rarely is an actual animal encountered. However, damage, paw and claw marks have been noted. A jungle cat was killed by a car on Hayling Island in 1988. In January 1994, national papers published pictures of a dead Asian leopard cat shot at Yaverland, Isle of Wight in 1987, which Messrs. S. Skinner and J. Ward had set a trap for, thinking it was a fox which was worrying their ducks; what they caught was a three and a-half foot spotted animal. These were tangible beasts.

ABC sightings on the Island are reported from as long ago as 1895. Incidents listed for the 1990's by the *Fortean Times* include that of an animal nicknamed "The Beast of Tweseldown", allegedly seen from ten feet at Fleet; a sighting by five people of an ABC attacking a collie and frightening ponies in the New Forest (searches by New Forest keepers and Lymington police proved fruitless; murky photographs were taken by two brothers from 30 yards near Tweseldown Racecourse of what purported to be the same animal); an ABC seen stalking a roe deer in Ayling Lane, Aldershot and several reported sightings since in the same area; a sighting at Old Basing from the M3 of an attack on two sheep; one opposite the house of Ron Kirby at Winchester attacking a deer and a 'Lion Hunt' at Basingstoke of a beast tracked with binoculars for several minutes by gamekeeper Mr. Lischcombes and positively identified as a lion. Lambs and ewes were savaged in Titchfield over a period of three years and a driver on the A343 near Abbott's Ann spotted what looked like a young male lion.

One's initial response to such stories is that the animals were escapees from zoos or private collections, or their descendants. The suggestion that something supernatural is occurring must stem from the elusive nature of the beasts. Why has it not been possible to catch one? Well, would you let yourself be caught by humans if you were an ABC? They must be very shy and wise enough to avoid our species.

Sensed especially by the cat ...

Mrs. Lambert once lived in an East Meon cottage which had been part of the New Inn's stables. Her cat would sometimes look up, startled, as if it sensed or saw something she could not. Mrs. Lambert slept downstairs and was frequently wakened by a draught from the door, which had opened in spite of her habitually bolting it from the inside before going to bed. One day, as a bricklayer was repairing her dining-room ceiling, he found a hidden heap of lace-bobbins between it and the floor above, which suggested the house was once a lacemaker's home. After she left the house, an inner door was found in a hollow wall with stairs leading to an attic in which were a pair of small sooty boots. The next occupants of the house, the Burleys, thought they must have been worn by a little Victorian sweep; some sweeps' steps were found to the old chimney. Of course, the house's history could have been unconnected with the opening door; but if it was, perhaps echoes of lives in the past had been sensed by the modern occupants, especially by the cat. What do you think?

Remnants of a haunting ...

Peter Underwood records that in Meonstoke no one was able to keep a dog at Meonstoke House, a building started in 1713 and added to. Its atmosphere affected dogs adversely. The Warners, who moved in in 1975, with their two children and a previously well-behaved old English sheepdog, were puzzled when it became agitated, tried to get out of the house in the daytime, whined at night and became upset in the hall. A doorbell inexplicably rang and a door on a landing would not remain closed at night. Sadly, they sent their pet to live on a farm, where the dog settled happily with strangers. Underwood sees the happenings at the house as "remnants of a haunting that has never come to light".

Ghost cat ...

In Emsworth High Street there is an Italian Restaurant, then Spencer's Restaurant, then a bakery (now the Petit Pain) and next door to that an old house which an Emsworth man told me reputedly has a ghost cat.

"Several people have seen it," he said, "and it has fights with other

81

cats." He had not actually seen it himself. The above story reminds me of times when our own cat, Nutmeg, appeared to be experiencing the paranormal. He had been brought up with one of our two dear Siamese since they were both kittens. After one of them was killed on the road our lonely Nutmeg, a Burmese, took to making noises on the landing which sounded remarkably like the characteristic cries of a Siamese. He had previously been rather a quiet cat. It was almost as if the Siamese had returned from a cat's heaven to be with his lonely friend. We assumed he was grieving and possibly conjuring up the memory of his lost companion for comfort, as people do. After a while, his Siamese-like cries became less heart-rending, he behaved more normally and attached himself to us for company.

Another occasion was quite different in its impact and appeared to us to have no explanation. We noticed Nutmeg was continually shying away from something we could not see. It was as if he had seen a ghost, or at least, something which was invisible to ourselves. He was not a happy cat.

Sceptical of a paranormal explanation we took him to see the vet, when the cat's dodging and shying started again next day, who asked about his diet.

"Conventional canned cat food mainly, with a little dried cat food and packeted semi-dried for occasional snacks, plus left-overs he is able scrounge from our own plates," we told him.

"Meat?" asked the vet.

"Well, yes," we said. "For instance, we made sandwiches from canned processed pork, mustard and cress for our own lunch and he polished off the remains of the pork ..."

"That's probably it," said the vet. He advised us not to give Nutmeg canned meat intended for human consumption as it often contained amounts of preservatives not good for cats, but harmless when diluted in the larger body-volume of human adults (whose diet is in any case mixed). Preservatives in the meat could have caused our cat to hallucinate. No wonder he looked sad and shied at his own shadow. We gave him no more canned meat scraps and he saw no more 'ghosts'. We think he still misses his Siamese companion, but with less pain as time passes. I know we do.

Animals are also mentioned in stories of haunted inns at the Robin Hood, Rowland's Castle and the Brushmakers' Arms, Upham (both page 28) and the Guardsman, Portsmouth (page 36).

CHILDREN, CHURCHES AND CHURCHYARDS

Child ghosts appear in stories elsewhere in this book at Bramshott Church, Arreton Manor, in the New Forest, at pubs at Wallington and Cadnam and at a house in East Meon, where the 'ghost' was possibly that of a little nineteenth century sweep (see chapter *Animals* and *Houses*). Traditionally children are more 'tuned in' to the supernatural than adults, an idea which may have arisen because children examine evidence less logically and more intuitively than adults in our culture. Very young children have to learn the difference between what is real and what takes place in their imagination as part of developing their thought processes. Certainly, many normal adults are known to have had imaginary companions as children - friends they talked to, played with and even insisted their parents set a place for at table, but whom nobody else could see. Not withstanding this, one still hears stories in which children are supposed to have sensed the supernatural when adults could not, which are very believable.

The reader may draw his own conclusions.

The following story was particularly interesting to me because in 1995 I was able to talk to four people who had experienced strange happenings in the same house. Some of them seem to have been mild poltergeist activity, but phantom children were seen by several witnesses and some of the movements of things were described as strange or mischievous rather than hostile. I report these conversations at length, so that the reader may draw his own conclusions.

Number 50 East Street, Havant, is almost opposite the old post office; it currently houses a dental practice where the two receptionists I spoke to said that they were not aware of any hauntings since the practice took over the house at least a year earlier and they had not heard of any previously. However, a Westbourne girl who worked in about 1979 for a firm occupying the premises - then Hair of London (hairdresser's) - told me of her weird experience in the 300-year-old listed building.

"I used to dog-sit in the flat there for two Afghan hounds and a dachshund of an evening. I was eighteen at the time," she said. "There were also two cats. One of the cats was by me and the other was out as I was watching *The Streets of San Francisco* on television, by myself except for the animals. Now, the owner of the flat had a heavy bust of a man - possibly Greek, I'm not sure - and a massive yucca-type plant, near the window. Both were very heavy and it took two people to move either of them. As I watched the programme, the plant fell over and the bust moved - it sort of swivelled - the cat's hackles rose and I checked the animals. One cat was still with me, the dogs were still in their bed in the kitchen, the other cat not there. The window was open, but there was no wind.

"I was petrified, waiting for the girl who lived in the flat to come home," she told me. "I couldn't understand how the heavy objects had moved by themselves. The only possible reasonable explanation was that one of the Post Office vans had driven into the yard at the back of the post office across the road and had somehow caused vibrations, yet that did not seem very likely." (The yard of the post office is down a side-street diagonally opposite number 50, but separated from it by the buildings on the corner. The theory about the Post Office vans seems unlikely to me too, unless there was a violent collision and this would presumably have been heard, even through the noise of the television.) The girl dog-sitter attempted to stand the plant up again but was unable to shift it.

Not long afterwards, she told me, the owner of the flat contacted a Leigh Park psychic, who is said to have felt four presences haunting the flat. One was an old lady, whom the owner assumed was a previous tenant. Another was a boy, possibly disturbed during renovations of the chimney. I spoke to the former owner of the premises, Mr. Graham Glanville-Cole, at his new work-place, Coiffeur, a hairdresser's in West Street, Havant, now known as Hair of London, West Street. He said:

"Things went on in the house over many years. I owned it for twenty years and in the early days did not realise anything was happening. Doors used to open and close at night - I became quite ill and was in hospital; my doctor thought I had been overworking. Then a local Methodist minister who was a customer came upstairs. He said there was 'something there' (something supernatural?). People - friends - used to feel a tugging; some used to fall on the stairs.

"A medium came. They think there was a fire in the premises next door (then a solicitor's) years ago, when a number of children got trapped. Debrah (his employee at both Hair of London, West Street and Coiffeur) saw a little girl on the top of the stairs. A visitor who knew nothing of the problem saw a child sitting at the top of the stairs - he looked for a child everywhere, said he didn't know we had one in the house - we hadn't at the time.

"Several times I tried to sell the house - I tried to get away from it. I've been left now three years and feel quite different about the direction of my life. My life's opened up. The situation at the house was engulfing me. I started to restore it to what it was, very stark, with Georgian furniture; I became obsessed ... I had an exorcism done once - it was okay for a while ... but then I got tired of doors opening and shutting; I took all the doors off ... it was mischievous things, nothing nasty. I wouldn't like to make anyone scared, but things moved. They were not taken; you just thought 'I know I didn't put that there...' Teddy bears and things, things a child would take a fancy to. My animals were not affected.

"Debrah lived in the flat. Lots of people wouldn't go up the stairs. Two of the girls (the hairdressers who worked there) stayed in the flat and left next morning much earlier than planned. A friend who was a singer brought her young brother to stay. In the morning he (the brother) said: 'Do you know, those children were talking all night?'

"There was a fire once and someone was killed. This was soon after I went to live in the house. I had thought it was that which gave me problems. I saw the doctor. When the medium came she said: 'There's smoke'. I told her: 'There was a fire; a tenant - an old woman - I pulled her out but she was already too far gone ...'

"But the medium said, 'No, not that. It's a spirit living here without any shadow of a doubt.'

"The house was old but when I was digging for the swimming pool, I found remains of the Roman settlement; so people have lived

85

there for a long time. It is not surprising if something clings from all those lives. No one was hurt by the haunting. It was just unnerving. When Debrah rented the flat she saw a young girl - it was uncanny. Others have seen a boy."

I talked to Debrah Reading who was working at Coiffeur when I called. She confirmed she had seen a little girl at the top of the stairs at number 50 East Street.

"I thought it was my daughter. I had just got out of the bath and looked up the stairs to tell her she could come and use the same bath water; that I'd finished. But my daughter was in the kitchen. I knew really, as soon as I properly looked up at the little girl on the stairs. She had a creamy-coloured long dress; it was old-fashioned, maybe Victorian (I can't really date it), with little satin pump-like ballet shoes; I remember the shoes, because one was trailing through the bannisters. The child was about seven." She added: "A friend saw the child in the early hours of the morning. She (the friend) was sleeping in my daughter's room and knew nothing of all this. Next morning she said to me 'Your daughter has been sitting on my bed'; but I knew my daughter was staying at my mother's." Debrah said she was not at all worried by the ghost; she was rather excited: "I rushed downstairs to tell Graham. He told me not to be idiotic."

She added that her colleagues Kerry and Simone (both hairdressers) heard music and drums. Kerry Dean of Stockheath Way, Leigh Park, confirmed that she and Simone had gone to stay at the flat and had "heard music and noises like children in a playground, and we were so scared we got into the same bed". Kerry added that next door to her own home a house was supposed to be haunted "by a friendly ghost". Things had moved. There was a young couple there now, though, and she didn't think they had been troubled.

I had to leave, for my husband was waiting for me in the car. There was obviously more happening in the Havant area than I had ever imagined.

Cousins and Rogers record that there was a serious fire in Havant in about 1760 when most of the present shopping area of West Street and parts of East and North Street were destroyed, but I have found nothing specific about a house fire at or next to number 50 East Street then or later. (I searched references to the activities of the local fire brigade at Havant Museum.) However, the date of the 1760 fire was within the period Mr. Cole tried to reconstruct in his refurbishment of number 50; and Debrah had been unable to date at all accurately the old-fashioned costume of the child on the stairs. In other stories, paranormal activity has been associated with alterations to old premises which it has been assumed have nudged a ghost into making its presence felt. Is it possible that alterations in this building disturbed spirits from the past?

All four observers described the same impressions ...

Joan Forman describes as "a strictly temporary haunting" the sighting, in East Meon by four dawdling 14-year-old schoolboys one January afternoon, of a woman's figure which came out of a house in Temple Lane. An old woman, a spiritualist, had died there in recent months; the house was in darkness and believed to be empty. In the fading light, they thought the figure was following them down the hill; they hid while it passed towards the river's bridge and each felt something weird had happened. Quickly they sped to their separate homes, where each parent realised that their lad was genuinely scared. It may be that the fading light affected the boys' interpretation of what was seen and that group panic set in, but it is noteworthy that all four observers described the same impressions.

Sometimes little children can see things other people can't ...

A man from Emsworth told me his aunt, who lives in the New Forest, told the family that she had "passed a ghost on the stairs". The family were amused because the stairs in her old cottage are narrow, almost too narrow for the aunt; there is no room for her to pass anyone solid. They joked that it must have been a very thin ghost. When his own child was very young, though, before he could explain what he was looking at, the young man and his wife found the lad staring at a wall in the same house and giggling. Their explanation: "sometimes little children can see things other people can't". The same Emsworth child, aged four, told his father when they were in an old fort in the Pyrenees that he saw a soldier with a red uniform, black boots and a tall hat.

"We've been trying to find out what uniforms they had in those forts," he added. "It was near Perpignan, where some of the last French to be there took refuge ..."

Old St Thomas's Church, Portsmouth: the 'haunt' of Springheel Jack
[See p. 13]

CHURCH AND
CHURCHYARD GHOSTS

Little girl in a poke bonnet

Bramshott is on the the old London-Portsmouth road (now off the busy A3). The church guide says the village is alleged to be the most haunted in England "having a large resident population of ghostly apparitions", the church itself being haunted by two ghosts. A little girl in a poke bonnet, who drifts through the churchyard wall, is thought to come from the Victorian period when most of the present church was built. Another, seen among the gravestones, is a conventional spectre in a white shroud.

She did not know who the lady was ...

At Exton I was told by the very busy cook at the Shoe, where we lunched on toasted sandwiches:

"A lady in white is supposed to walk around the churchyard at night". She did not know who the lady was nor why she walked.

Her manor-house demolished, just to spite her...

The area around Hartley Mauditt church is reputed to be haunted. All that remains of the manor cellar is reputed to be connected by a passage to Selbourne Priory. The ghost is supposed to be that of Lady Stawell, sad because her unpleasant husband had her manor-house home demolished, just to spite her according to hearsay.

Straw hat and a pigtail ...

A pigtailed sailor with a straw hat (one of Nelson's men?) sometimes takes a pew at the west end of St. Peter's Church, Hayling, or so they say. A retired Hayling clergyman told me several people claimed to have seen him.

The wildlife is at ease ...

You remember that one of Dame Alicia Lisle's haunts is supposed to be near the church at Dibden? We met Mr. Martin Hall-Patch of Dibden Purlieu in Dibden churchyard, where he was cutting the grass.

"No one I know has seen the ghost [of Lady Alicia]," he said; "but then, I'm rarely here at dusk, when one would expect ... " He continued to cut the grass, then looked up and stopped for a moment or two – "but I'm always catching glimpses out of the corner of my eye... it may be a stone or something glimmering ... there's a feeling, a sense of something in the area; it's a sensation 'now was it that gravestone or something else?' I went to a Roman Catholic boarding school which was once a Benedictine monastery. There was always a sense of spirits roaming ... there's a sense here of spirits but they are at ease and at rest ... I like the oddity that, when I'm mowing or strimming, the birds never stop singing. It is comforting that the wildlife is at ease. Animals do sense things; cats, dogs and wildlife have no problems here. There may be more than one spirit; I don't know."

Animals can be ghosts, too: a ghostly white pig is said to appear in fields near Bramshott church.

90

SOUNDS, SMELLS AND HOSPITAL HAUNTINGS.

Sounds and smells feature in a number of ghost stories; sometimes they are the only indication of a haunting, according to those who sense these things.

Music, perfume and a woman's voice ...

In 1665 Charles II moved court to Winchester to escape a plague epidemic in London. The story that he lodged Nell Gwynne at the Deanery in St. Peter's Street is thought to be fabrication; but Nell was a frequent visitor at Farnborough Place (now St. Peter's Junior School, Farnborough). She was a guest of the Annesley family, who owned the house, which was later restored in Queen Anne's reign, from 1652. Her ghost is said to have been seen there occasionally. Some have reported "a creepy feeling", the perfume of roses and the sound of a harp, plus a woman's "divinely pretty" voice. (No one has mentioned oranges!)

Mr. Albert Bailey describes in the *Hampshire* magazine (December 1966) his searching beneath the house (when it was used as a hotel, shortly after the 2nd World War) for a tunnel believed to lead to the church crypt nearby. He experienced fear and cold, followed by whispering, music, perfume and a woman's voice reciting a short poem; he was no longer afraid. A caretaker had had the same intense fear in the same spot but had not stayed for the artistic performance! Former headmaster at the school, Mr. Howard Newton told Fox in 1992 that he saw nothing unusual but he experienced a cold, shivery

Odiham Castle: an atmospheric place haunted by King John's minstrel [see opposite]

The Pest House, another of Odiham's relics of the past

feeling in one room and an atmosphere of unease. Mr. Newton found that others had reported similar experiences and a couple of people had actually seen a ghost. A bishop had performed an exorcism before the school had moved into the building.

The smell of tom-cat usually lingers longer than that ...

Ms. Forman tells of "a strange fragment of a haunting" in a Regency house built on the site of Romsey Abbey Nunnery. It was the strong smell of tom-cats, noticed by the son of the house, then by his mother, in May 1977 in their dining-room, whose doors and windows had been closed all day, making it inaccessible to the animals. The mother also scented another smell, that of "a dirty old tramp", in the passage. They closed the doors and returned ten minutes later to find both smells gone. That the smell of tom-cat usually lingers longer than that led Ms. Forman to suspect a paranormal cause for the phenomenon.

Alton church porch is reported to be inexplicably perfumed with Lily of the Valley from time to time. A wandering minstrel is said to haunt King John's Castle at Odiham. We did not see him on our visit there, or hear his music; it was such a cold, damp day we were loathe to wait for him to appear. The castle, reached via a path along the Basingstoke Canal, has an atmosphere though.

The scent of incense is part of the Arreton Manor ghost story and perfume features in the haunting story of Bramshill. Mr. Adams, an Elizabethan gamekeeper, is reputed to smoke his pipe outside his cottage at Bramshott.

Shaw (1892) wrote of ghostly bells which rang from Stenbury, a vanished village near Preston Candover. Bells from an ancient church off South Hayling, which local legend says was inundated by a great flood in 1341, are said to be heard sometimes on the island.

A phantom boy with a flute is described in the chapter "Ghosts of Road and Railway" (page 20) and ghostly scents are mentioned elsewhere in this volume, at Quarry Road, Winchester, ("Monastic Ghosts" chapter, page 39), and in the chapter "Spirited Inns", at the George and Falcon, North Warnford (page 27) and at Julie's Restaurant, Emsworth.

A grey lady, said to be Miss Nightingale's ghost ...

94

HOSPITAL HAUNTINGS

I used to work in the Leeds General Infirmary. Its corridors were distinctly spooky at night or when smog penetrated the basement, where it took courage to walk even when one told oneself firmly one did not believe in ghosts.

According to nurses to whom I have spoken, many nursing establishments have a 'Grey Lady' who glides noiselessly down corridors or walks the wards. Here are several Hampshire hospital ghost stories and one vague haunting of a former old folks' home.

A grey lady, said to be Miss Nightingale's ghost ...

Florence Nightingale campaigned for military hospitals to be built on practical lines with wards separated to prevent cross-infection, but plans for Netley Hospital so appalled her that she lobbied her neighbour, the then Prime Minister, Lord Palmerston of Broadlands, to get them changed. Although she wielded considerable power through contacts with influential people and knew very well what she was talking about, from experience and study, her views were ignored by the military (she was not their favourite person). The hospital foundation stone was laid in March 1863 by Queen Victoria and the huge building used for the wounded of the Boer War and both World Wars. In 1950 it became the army's principal psychiatric hospital. Before its eventual demolition in 1966, inexplicably, the ghost of Miss Nightingale was supposed to be trying to prevent its destruction. I should have thought her ghost would have been jubilant that the military had eventually realised the hospital was a white elephant; she would have recognised the irony of it all having taken so long …

Notwithstanding the above, an unidentified Grey Lady, said by some to be Miss Nightingale's ghost, was for years supposed to haunt Netley Hospital and was seen by a number of reliable people. At one time it was almost treated as a military secret; it was considered awfully bad for morale to have a Grey Lady around the place who reputedly appeared before a death.

There were plenty of deaths in early military hospitals through cross-infection, a fact established beyond doubt by Miss Nightingale, whose observations and studies in Britain and Europe were the basis for changes in hospital building and administration at the end of the nineteenth and beginning of the twentieth centuries.

Netley hospital was so big that, whenever the Grey Lady was noticed, it was likely to be before some death or other, bearing in mind the horrors of being wounded on the field of battle before the advent of antibiotics. During her work in the Crimea the Lady with the Lamp (the real, not the ghostly, Miss Nightingale) had made a point of being with wounded men who were not expected to survive the night. Perhaps these many acts of compassion contributed in military circles to stories of her haunting of Netley hospital.

Some say the Grey Lady was a nurse who threw herself from the roof when a patient with whom she fell in love died. Stephen Darby (*circa* 1900) wrote that a nursing sister had thrown herself off the roof after poisoning her lover, a patient, whom she found in another nurse's arms. Yet another version was that the unfortunate girl had been upset after giving a patient an accidental drug overdose.

Darby recorded that Alice Mawcombe saw the Lady on a visit to her brother in 1878. I do not know how long the brother survived the visit; he certainly won't be alive now! A Mr. Whittaker of Bitterne, serving with the R.A.M.C. in 1936, claimed he saw a figure which he assumed to be the Night Sister; she "passed into nothing". He had heard that when the Grey Lady walked, a patient would die. Four hours later, a patient with a distressing cough did die. A night telephonist at the hospital told a relative that he and his colleagues had also seen the Grey Lady, usually in the ground floor main corridor. Death was not associated with these sightings.

Was it possible that, reliable folk as they were, they misinterpreted visual cues in poor light? Even that they were subconsciously influenced by ghost stories they had heard? I told the Grey Lady of Netley story

Netley Abbey, resplendent in its ruined splendour

Old lock up in Warblington churchyard, to deter body-snatchers

to a former nurse, who clicked her tongue and said, "Night duty is notorious. It can be quite stressful."

As Netley hospital was being demolished in 1966, reporters from the *Evening Echo,* with the contractor whose workmen had been frightened by a drifting figure, searched the building, heard "a deep piano chord" and saw a woman in an old-fashioned nurse's uniform walk slowly and silently away from them to vanish down a side passage. They did not follow, but later found an old piano in the building. If this was a hoax, said the pressman who wrote up the story that Halloween, it was "exceptionally well done". The Royal Chapel, a remnant of the formerly grandiose hospital building, is now part of a country park.

The Cambridge Military Hospital Grey Lady ...

The Cambridge Military Hospital, Aldershot, has a legend, written of in a 1974 history of the hospital, of a Grey Lady said to haunt the women's ward and to be the ghost of a sister in the Queen Alexandra Imperial Nursing Service. It is reputed she accidentally gave a fatal overdose to a patient, then threw herself over a hospital balcony to her death. Patients and staff used to see her doing ward rounds as in life, usually in the vicinity of Ward 13 (which did have a balcony at one time). An appearance was recorded in 1969. She has been said to have appeared as a comforting presence when staff were under pressure. (The hospital closed in about 1995.)

This story bears some similarity to that of the Grey Lady of Netley. Oddly, Peter Underwood of the Ghost Club admits his wife was once mistaken for the Grey Lady of Cambridge Military Hospital whilst visiting a friend!

Seen walking the wards at Haslar Naval Hospital ...

Haslar Naval Hospital, known since April 1997 as the Royal Hospital, Haslar, for it now serves all three of the armed services, is at the entrance to Portsmouth Harbour in Gosport.

In the early hours of one morning in 1814, I'm told, a sentry paced up and down at the main gate of this establishment. Suddenly he stopped, for, from the darkness ahead, came a hooded figure which glowed red through the gloom. The sentry froze, then he ran from his post screaming. He is said to have died half an hour later as a result of his terror; what a waste of a young life! What a pity, too, because he had not seen a ghost but a nurse who was hurrying to an urgent case outside the hospital! To keep warm, she had wrapped herself in a red cloth and carried her candle close to her chest but beneath the cloak, not realising how ghostly her appearance appeared as she passed through the hospital gates.

Although the above does not involve a 'real' ghost, (and may be only a cautionary tale told to rookie sentries), several sightings over the years have not been explained. Hearsay is that nursing sisters from the nineteenth century have been seen roaming the grounds of the hospital during the dark hours and that others have been sighted walking the wards. One story concerns a male patient in a psychiatric ward who fell in love with one of the young nurses. She returned his love but the hospital authorities refused them permission to marry. In despair, he hanged himself in the ward and she, distraught, threw herself down the lift shaft (which makes a change from the usual balcony). It is said (but always by someone who has heard it from someone else) that on certain nights her screams can be heard penetrating the still night air, and that on occasion the silhouette of a man swinging by the neck from a rope has been seen too. Whether there is a grain of truth in this story, I know not; I suspect it to be an exercise of macabre naval humour.

Music from a room with no radios ...

Foresters, in Hythe, is an old building which was a residential home for elderly folk but is now a holiday centre. Jo Baker, the manager, told me it is reputedly haunted by "the proverbial Grey Lady", but that personally she has her doubts, as every establishment she has ever worked in that's an old building has had one. Staff have reported to her a presence which they feel is there.

"It makes people jump," she added; "even our project director, on her own at night, was affected by an eerie feeling when doors banged inexplicably."

"Has any of your staff actually seen anything?" I asked.

"I don't know," she replied. "They've given up telling me about it. They know I'm sceptical. I just told them not to alarm the guests; but if there is one, it is a friendly ghost - music from a room with no radios - things like that. There is no need for anyone to be alarmed."

Earlier I had spoken to a former employee at Foresters. She was convinced the place was haunted and said she had experienced "a creepy feeling" there. She had, however, been told by other members of staff that there was a ghost. Had the existing staff told the story in order to scare the new person in their midst, I wondered? Many groups of people have "joining rituals", such as the sending of a new worker to stores for "a long wait" - cruel in my view, but it happens. The new employee was convinced this was not so, as those who professed to have heard or sensed the ghost seemed "quite genuine". Some were mildly scared, but concerned not to alarm the clients. This vague and friendly spectre appears to have been reported by a number of people, and those who feel it to be there have learned to live with it.

The evil Cockatrice: one such beast harrassed the nuns of Wherewell Abbey [see page 104]

A MIX OF MYTH, LEGEND AND HISTORY.

Some stories of early times in Hampshire and Sussex are impossible to unravel from myth and legend; tales are told in several versions of which any one could be true, partly true or a complete fabrication. I have not attempted to unravel the following but they are part of the heritage of the area and as such worth recording here.

Andover was noted in the past as the site of a residence of the West Saxon kings, and William the Conqueror established a priory there. Legend says that a priest was struck dead whilst conducting mass on Christmas Eve, 1171, in the town, and that the other priests present were not harmed but saw a beast the shape of a pig running around their feet. This story sounds to me like propaganda by one political group to discredit another, or by uncharitable rivals to discredit a dead priest who could no longer defend himself; but I don't really know. What do you think?

Edmund and Cnut fought a battle west of Andover, according to Shore; Cnut's barrow was said to lie midway along the line of a four mile underground path from Danebury to Quarely hill forts. Danebury today is an ideal place to take a group of children on a summer birthday picnic so long as you don't lose them in the dense vegetation towards the middle.

The spirit of William Rufus (William II of England) is said to haunt the Rufus Stone (New Forest) where he died on August 2nd 1100 AD, traditionally on a stag hunt in which he was unintentionally shot in the chest by an arrow from Walter Tyrell's bow. Alternative explanations of the king's death include murder by one or other of the hunters, or by more than one of them in collusion. Whatever happened prior to the arrow incident, the hunters at once fled. One, the king's brother, Henry, at once went to claim the crown of England in Winchester; another, William of Breteuil, followed, to counterclaim the crown for his eldest son, Robert. Walter Tyrell left hurriedly for Normandy, which he might well have done, even had the killing of the king been accidental. William's body was found where it fell by Purkis the charcoal-burner and brought to Winchester on his farm cart, after which it was buried in Winchester Cathedral.

They say hereabouts that on the anniversary of Rufus's death his restless ghost follows the bloody trail of Purkis's cart between Stony Cross and Cadnam and that Ocknell Pond, west of the Rufus Stone, runs red where Walter Tyrell washed (royal?) blood from his hands before mounting a horse with reversed shoes. He did this in order to disguise his tracks to the coast, and an uncomfortable journey for both horse and man it must have been. A legend connected with William Rufus's ghost says that at Cadnam an oak sprouted leaves on old Christmas day; I do not know where exactly the oak was.

The New Forest is also supposed to have little people, known as pixies, in certain parts of it. They are seen fleetingly out of the eye corner. I haven't met one yet. I wonder whether they are related to the garden gnomes, of which we saw so many in the Isle of Wight ... In wild areas of the Forest, invisible somethings are said to affect both wild beasts and people ... "a groaning tree" in the southern part was investigated so thoroughly it was cut down to see why it made so much noise and no one was any the wiser.

Farquharson-Coe describes how one of the Lords Montague married towards the end of last century and had five daughters. When a son was at last born to them to inherit the estate, a flock of swans rose from the lake at Beaulieu and flew round the house in welcome.

A lovely story noted in various parts of Hampshire in the past is that the cattle all knelt there on Christmas Eve at midnight. There was a custom in the Middle Ages of holding a service called the Office of the Shepherds in certain churches on Christmas Eve, during which shepherds brought their sheep into church, having taught them to kneel at the altar. Maybe the story of the kneeling cattle grew from that.

Bishop Swithun of Winchester died in 862 AD and was buried outside the church at his own request so the rain would fall on him. However, the monks decided to move him to a prestigious tomb inside the church. Legend says his spirit was so angry that his remains should be moved against his wishes that he made it rain for 40 days, until the monks decided to leave him be. Henceforth, if it rained on St.Swithun's day (July 15th) it was considered an omen of a long spell of wet weather. It still is, half in jest. English weather is relatively unpredictable still, in spite of long-range weather-forecasting and satellite pictures of swirling clouds on television.

At South Baddersley the Danes' Stream, which runs through iron-bearing soil, is nevertheless said to run red with the blood of Danes killed there over 1000 years ago.

Near Botley, on the outskirts of Southampton, a witch called Kit Nox was supposed to become airborne from time to time.

One of the heroes of Old Southampton was Sir Bevis, who legend says killed the giant Ascapart. The giant at the time was laying waste the surrounding countryside, as giants did in those days. Sir Bevis's statue is at Southampton Bargate. Ascapart's skeleton is believed to lie beneath a tumulus called the Bevis Mound.

A mediaeval legend attributes the village name Rowland's Castle, north of Havant, to the slaying of the Saracen giant Angalouffe, who had been laying waste the land locally, by someone called Rowland, in what is now the village. This story is remarkably similar to that of Sir Bevis above. Some say Rowland was one of the same race of giants as Sir Bevis of Southampton. (The version of the Sir Bevis story I read had not mentioned that he was a giant too.) There are traces of a castle noted on the ordnance survey map and Norman flints in the building of a large house named Deer Leap at Rowland's Castle. Access has been sought for the public to be able to visit the castle mound. Some people are convinced that the first part of the name of their village means "land of the Roe deer". The earliest version of the name probably means Red Lakes in Celtic and indicates the place was a Celtic settlement before a later Norman castle was built, with marshy ground as part of its defences.

Traces of a Saxon Priory remain at Wherewell. Tradition says the priory was founded by Queen Elfrida in sorrow for having murdered her stepson Edward at Corfe Castle. She did this in order to set her own child on the throne but was tormented by evil spirits, one of which, a monstrous fiend, threatened to drag her down in the night. (Guilty conscience, I shouldn't wonder, and if it wasn't it should have been.) We found no priory remains when we went to look for them, but it is said that the site of the old priory is haunted by nuns who carry candles and that the place in the grounds where the nuns were buried (over the churchyard wall) is sometimes lit by lights. In 1997, archaeologists discovered the remains of a very large building, assumed to be Wherewell Priory.

A superstition in the village against eating ducks' eggs is said to have sprung up because a duck egg laid long ago beneath the priory was sat on by a toad. A cockatrice hatched from the egg and grew gigantic. Now the thing you should know about the mythical cockatrice in order to appreciate this story fully is that its gaze is deadly, so those who look into its eyes die. One version of the tale says the beast remained in the vault where it was hatched, grew, then killed everyone who approached it until a man thought of dangling a mirror into the vault where it lay. It attacked its reflection and while thus diverted was killed by the anonymous hero. Another says the nuns fed the beast in a specially built den but were jolly careful not to look directly at it, as they knew of the reputation of its kind for possessing an evil eye and for biting the hand that fed it; the beast escaped and a number of nuns were killed. It was, however, outwitted by Green the woodcutter, to whom the remaining nuns had appealed for help. Green tracked the animal down and set a mirror before it. The mirror being bright but the animal on the dull side, it fought with its reflection and as it did so was slain by Green, who had craftily waited for this moment, at what is now known as Green's copse.

Chilbolton Rectory is reputed to be haunted by a nun who ran off from St. Cross Abbey.

Dragon Lane, Bisterne, is all that is left of the legendary dragon which lived on Burley Beacon. The villagers gave it milk on request (this dragon could talk?) to save their sheep, for the dragon was partial to roast lamb; remember, dragons have very hot breath so need no gas ovens. When the sheep supply ran out, reasoned the villagers, the dragon would have to vary his menu. Thus, fearing for their own safety and that of their children and pigs, they hired a knight who craftily covered himself in birdlime as insulation from the dragon's fiery breath. It would never do, thought the knight, sensibly enough, for him to be roasted alive and therefore unable to spend the hiring fee.

I understand that knights of old were none too particular about personal hygiene, being sewn into their garments once or twice a year. Nevertheless, after he had fought and killed the dragon, as per contract, hopefully he had a bath. I think he was very brave to anoint himself with birdlime, let alone tackle the hungry dragon.

Charles Dickens is reputed to have stayed at Yew Tree House, Broughton. A Mrs. Whicher who lived there is said to be the origin of the character Miss Havisham in *Great Expectations*. Next to the house grew two large yew trees called Esau and Jacob; a curse was supposed to fall on the village if they were ever destroyed. However, one of them was felled in 1984 because it had become dangerous and no mishap occurred.

Druid priests are supposed to have sacrificed white bulls at Mottistone, Isle of Wight, beside the two long stones said to represent a perpendicular god and a horizontal goddess. The name Mottistone (Old English) suggests this was a meeting place.

Legend says that if you open the door of the Church of St. Margaret's, East Wellow, and look at Saint Christopher carrying the Christ-child, you are safe for the day. Florence Nightingale is buried at East Wellow; she lived at nearby Embley Park.

A grampus lived in an old yew tree in Highclere churchyard. Like all other grampi it was a dolphin-like beast, more used to marine life than to the quiet of a country churchyard. Bored out of its mind, therefore, it breathed so heavily it annoyed the villagers, who were not too pleased, either, when it chased them. A priest banished it to the Red Sea for 1000 years, but the date of this exorcism is lost so it is not known when it will come back (so listen out for heavy breathing in Highclere churchyard). Of course, with luck it might prefer a warmer climate and settle abroad for good, then you need not worry.

Marwell Hall, Owlesbury, is said to be haunted by the ghost of Jane Seymour, whom Henry VIII secretly married there while his previous wife, Anne Boleyn, was in the Tower of London waiting to be executed. Jane died a year later in childbirth (her baby survived to become Edward VI of England). Jane's rival's ghost is said to walk the avenue of yews in the grounds of Marwell (when it is not busy haunting the Tower of London, that is).

When plague struck the village of Vernham Dean the villagers heroically agreed, on advice from their rector, to isolate themsleves on a hill. He promised to bring them food. One story says the rector was too scared to take them the promised provisions; another that he died of plague before he could do so, which seems more likely, knowing the virulence of the epidemic. Whatever the reason, those of his flock not dying of plague are said to have done so from starvation, and a clerical ghost forever haunts the path to the hill.

A man whose boyhood home was in Meonstoke spoke of the belief there that, at Old Winchester Hill nearby (an Iron Age hillfort), Winchester was going to be built but the buildings got damaged again and again until in the end the king, or whatever, built the city on its present site instead. Old Winchester Hill was the preferred site because of its commanding position - wide views and so on. He could tell me no more about the legend and said,
"The old folk knew, but they're in the churchyard."
Who, I asked, were supposed to have damaged the buildings?
"The people who were there before," he said.
"Real people? Kelpies? Ghosts?" I asked.
"I can't tell you anymore. Ask about in Meonstoke. Somebody may be able to tell you."
So one day my husband and I set off for the Meon Valley to "ask about", in search of pixies.
At the Buck's Head nothing was known, but "Ask the girl in the post office" we were told; "she'd know. She's local." They knew about Roman excavations at Meonstoke one summer. (Were the "old people" Romans?)

The girl in the post office and several customers were most interesting on the subject of Roman remains. They were unsure of the date; it had been excavated at least twice. They'd found the whole end of a Roman house, which had been knocked down in one piece.

We found out about the excavations from Mr. Bruce Horn on whose farm they had taken place. It was true a Roman house end had been found intact. It was an exciting find but nothing to do with pixies.

Someone came into the shop who had heard of the Pixie legend. Who, I asked, were the people who were supposed to have "knocked the houses down"? Before the Romans, they thought, someone had started to build a city. The Meon Valley Pixies pulled it all down. They were the old people, there were barrows and things on the hill - the people who were there before. They used to say if the Meon Valley Pixies didn't like you, a lot of things went wrong, you moved out and didn't settle. Two families moved out in the 1940's or 1950's.

"Well, we've been here for years and awful things have happened from time to time," said one woman "and we've stayed. We like it here. But I have heard of people who have moved out; didn't fit into country life, I daresay."

Had I heard of the Wyndham's Curse? The Wyndhams of Corhampton House (now flats known as Wyndham Lodge) had a son who wanted to marry a gypsy girl. He was disinherited but the marriage went ahead. The curse was that they would never have a male heir and they didn't. "She is buried in the churchyard," I was told; "the young Mrs. Wyndham." What a romantic, sad story. Part of the mystery of Meonstoke, but what about the pixies?

Much of Meonstoke was destroyed by fire in the 1600's, they said; and a cottage next to the church was thatched and burned down on Guy Fawkes night (in the early 1990's, they thought; "time just kaleidoscopes here"). Were the Pixies held responsible for this disaster too, I wondered? One of the women said it was a boiler caused the fire, or so it was said. The pixies remained elusive.

I have found no written reference to the Meon Valley Pixies. They may be related to the little people of the New Forest. I was told in Droxford of a couple of people who might tell me more, wrote to one of them, but have had no reply. I concluded the Pixies were secretive souls whom Meon Valley folk prefer to keep to themselves. If any reader can tell me more about them without incurring their displeasure or that of their neighbours, I'd be glad to hear.

Nineteenth century country lore in Hampshire was that patients could be cured of otherwise incurable maladies by being drawn through an ash tree. A young tree was split for the purpose of this uncomfortable ritual.

Legend says Silchester was the destination of King Gurmond with 160,000 Africans who landed at Southampton after he had defeated Ireland; a curious legend; where did they go after that? (Shades of the *Pied Piper?*)

Silchester and its Roman Wall: what became of Gurmond and his Africans?

GHOSTS KNOW NO BOUNDARIES ...

Ghosts know no boundaries. Whilst researching *Hampshire Hauntings*, the following stories have been related to me about happenings over the Hampshire border, mostly in Sussex, or things which happened elsewhere to Hampshire people (I count Christchurch as Hampshire, because it once was; also the Isle of Wight, which is now independent; is this perverse?) They are too good to leave out, so here they are.

I could not believe my eyes ...

During the 1980's Mrs. Isomer Bruce of Ryde, Isle of Wight, went on a coach tour holiday with her husband to Torquay. On the Tuesday they were taken to Plymouth where there was to be an optional boat trip on the River Tamar. The day was on the chilly side, so as the couple had not brought macs or heavy coats with them they remained perfectly happily on a seat whilst the rest of their party sailed up the river. They enjoyed looking out to sea and watching the passers-by stroll to and fro beside the sea wall. Then, Mrs. Bruce says:

"Suddenly, I could not believe my eyes ... out of the crowd a tall gentlemen wearing a dark coat, hat and suit came towards us. He stood in front of us and just looked at us, penetrating our very souls. I was glued to the seat. My husband and I could hardly speak to each other and I still feel petrified when I think about it."

The man left them and went back to merge among the strolling pedestrians. Mr. and Mrs. Bruce believe this person to have been their brother-in-law, who had been dead for some years. Mrs. Bruce asks if I can explain the event. I can't. She adds:

"How could he possibly know we would be there, as our home was in Ryde?"

It looked like a big black dog

Ms. Debbie Twine of Northbrook Close, Buckland, Portsmouth, writes of an experience she and her family had in North Yorkshire 14 years ago, when she was 14 years old. She and her older sister, then 21, had gone with her sister's older friend, her brother, his wife and three young children plus his wife's parents, to stay in an old country house called Dixieland on the moors "miles from the farmer who owned the place and anywhere else". There were no street lights or lights from passing traffic as a long private road led to the house, opposite which were unused barns with dead birds on the floor inside. Debbie's sister's friend occupied one bedroom with her sister and the two youngest children (aged about seven and nine), while Debbie and the 12-year-old child were in a room facing the barns. The sister's friend's brother and his wife were in the room opposite her sister; the grandparents were downstairs. During a storm on the third night, Debbie and the 12-year-old could not sleep so moved into her sister's room, the child to sleep on the spare bed and Debbie in a made-up bed on the floor; there she fell asleep.

She woke in the middle of the night to see "a bright glowing light hovering over the 12-year-old; it was the shape of a person but had no features". She watched it for about four minutes then fell back to sleep. Next morning she told everyone what she had seen and they asked the farmer if there were any ghosts. He said "people had seen things", and that the house was supposed to be haunted by Oliver Cromwell's soldiers; campers on the moors had heard people marching past their tents at night.

Debbie's party found coloured light bulbs in the house and a small patch of blood on the floor of one of the rooms; they wondered whether the farmer and his friends had been holding seances.

The next night, Debbie and the 12-year-old again slept in her sister's room. This time, they all "heard moaning coming from an outside wall then stones being thrown against the window", writes Debbie. (Rather solid sounds for a ghost to make; could this have been hailstones?) The stone-throwing continued for about six minutes then stopped completely. Surprisingly, "everyone managed to get to sleep". Debbie was just dozing off (now in her sister's bed, because she

110

was so scared), when she looked ahead into the room where the married couple were sleeping and "saw a thing shaped like a dog lying on the settee, with bright red eyes staring at me. I woke my sister and she also saw it. It didn't move at all, but definitely looked like a big black dog." They eventually slept, thinking themselves lucky to be leaving the house soon. They heard nothing strange the following night.

The married couple had their two small dogs with them and, thinking they were hearing their animals running about, the night Debbie reports having seen the "big black dog", they had told them to get back into their baskets. However, when they looked for them the dogs were fast asleep; so who or what had made the dog footsteps, asks Debbie?

The day the holiday-makers were due to leave the house, the husband was packing all their belongings into the minibus when the others "heard rowing and swearing outside". The farmer and two other men were blocking up the barns with planks of wood and "were mocking my sister's friend's husband" as he prepared to drive. As Debbie's party boarded the minibus ready to go, the hostile men surrounded them, "still shouting and laughing and waving hammers about in their hands". The driver quickly drove off and they went home.

Debbie says she could not sleep for a week, thinking about this experience; she cannot remember a time when she has felt so scared. She believed in ghosts before this, but never wanted to see one. She adds that it was weird that the 12-year-old, over whom she had seen the glowing person-shape hover, was afterwards affected by "a mystery illness" and could not walk for a time. She ends her account: "I never want to see another ghost again." Was this a haunting or some unkind trickery? What was in the boarded-up barn? As Debbie and her group left Dixieland, their minibus passed another car load of people driving towards the house. She wonders whether they had a similarly relaxing break, away from it all ... Me, I wonder what went on in the barn and doubt whether Cromwell's men had anything to do with it, whatever it was.

She asked her husband to check the wiring ...

A young couple moved into the wife's mother's house in Westbourne, on the Hampshire-Sussex border. The widowed mother lived with them for about six months, then moved out to a new home. The girl told me that when her husband was out on a night shift she smelt smoke. She checked their cooking and heating appliances to see if she had inadvertently left something switched on. All was well, except that she could still smell smoke. She asked her husband to check the wiring. The wiring was in order. She realised the smell was tobacco smoke.

"We don't smoke, Mum doesn't (although Dad did) and the man next door said he didn't smoke either. The smoke smell only occurred after Mum moved out. I thought it was my father and that he was cross that we were in the house and that she wasn't there, although of course she had gone to her new home because she wanted to ... I talk to him sometimes, you know, maybe if I've disagreed about something with my husband, I go into another room and say: 'Well, if you're there, I hope you are on my side!' " She found the idea of her father being there rather comforting, a gentle, happy haunting if haunting it be. She still isn't sure what to think.

A young Petworth woman told me that as a child of nine she had seen the apparition of a man in a mirror. The experience had frightened her very much but had not harmed her. Asked to describe the apparition she said "he was black and there was no one in the room really".

I put the light on and there's nothing there ...

I spoke to a lady who now lives near Chichester, West Sussex, about an unexplained experience which has followed her around the country.

"I don't believe in ghosts or anything," she assured me; "but it happens sometimes - once a month or more – it's sometimes in the bedroom. I'll be lying in bed and the side of the bed goes down, as if someone is sitting there. I can feel it's at the side of the bed - something. It started in Yorkshire at an old house I lived in, then it happened in a new house in the Isle Of Wight, at a new house in London and now in my new home (near Chichester). I get a bit scared sometimes; I put the light on and there's nothing there. I have never seen anything but I've started putting a little stool at that side of the bed, to stop this happening. I can never sleep on that side of the bed; it's a double bed."

112

"Does it work?" I asked; "I mean, does putting the stool there stop the bed going down as if something is there?"

"It has so far," she said. (This lady would rather not be named.)

A man in a trilby hat ...

Mr. and Mrs. Hedges used to live at Shipley Hill, North Chapel, Sussex. One night in April in the 1950's Mrs. Hedges awoke to see a man in a trilby hat at the end of the bed she shared with her husband.

"But my husband didn't see him," she adds. The stranger was "an ordinary, tall man; he had clothes on", she added hastily. "He was wearing an overcoat and he was not a young man. I can't tell you who he was or anything about him but it was a ghost, wasn't it? It's a long time ago and I only just thought of it when you asked us if we'd had any ghostly experiences." Her experience had worried neither her nor her husband and had not been repeated.

Another coach and horses

At Chapel, Sussex, several road accidents have been attributed to drivers having seen a phantom coach and horses which "comes from a wood between the two lodges and goes across the road". Mr. Hedges says that, years ago, the carriageway used to run straight across at this point.

The dog was going absolutely mad ...

Mr. David Hill, then publican at the Wheatsheaf, Chichester, had lived in a 110- year-old house in Collier Avenue, North Binsted for less than a year when I spoke to him in April 1995. He said that the previous summer he had been "washing the car and the dog" in his front garden when a couple came by who had known the previous owners of the house. "Have you seen the ghost yet?" they asked. He had not. They explained that the former occupants had been sensitive to the supernatural and were sure there was a ghost there. Their child had been terrified. They asked if he had not felt "the cold". He replied that he never did and had not had the heating on since he arrived. He thought no more about it until his girlfriend said there was "something about the house" and that she felt a distinct chill in the air there.

"Now, one night she woke about 3.00 am.," he went on. "She told me afterwards that a tiny bell was ringing and the dog was going absolutely mad. She thought it was something supernatural. I was under the duvet; I slept through the lot, never heard a thing. I've not seen nor heard anything that could have been a ghost all the time I've lived there. Maybe she's sensitive to such things."

Just over Hampshire's western border, about ten years ago, Mr. Gerald Durrant of Tuckton, Christchurch, was with his wife, driving their son home along the road opposite Hurn Airport, when he had a strange experience. He says:

"I have never checked out whether Hurn Airport was ever military, but we used to be lumbered as a 'taxi' service when our son Alistair was 17. One evening - it wasn't late - we were collecting him from somewhere when in front of me, on a ramshackle pushbike, was a fellow in a faded R.A.F. outfit.

" 'I nearly knocked that bloke down!' I gasped. We were by the Alice in Wonderland Maze. It (the cyclist) went across the car and made me swerve. At first I thought it was a person. My wife looked back and said there was nothing there."

Was it a road ghost? A trick of the light? The ghost of an airman stationed nearby in earlier times? His description of the apparition is fairly specific.

Mr. Durrant also tells me that he saw a ghost while on National Service in Colchester, in May, 1958:

"I was returning from taking a girl-friend home to the married quarters where her parents lived and took a short cut to Minden Barracks. I thought I'd reached the main road quickly, as I saw a circle of light. As I got towards it, the light started to shimmer. I felt the hair on the back of my neck rise. I passed an old air raid shelter and saw the seated figure of a soldier. He was dressed more like a First World War soldier than ... it was not like the battle dress I had on. He was smoking a pipe. I started to run in panic in the direction I thought was the barracks. At the bar into the barracks, instead of halting and checking in, I leap-frogged it (I was not stopped). I was eighteen. I had to report the next day to my superiors. I told them what I had seen. They didn't believe me. After that night, I stuck to the main road!"

Had the long-dead Cavalier come back to haunt us?

When my children were young we lived in Dorset. Now, a former family member had acquired from his deceased relative's effects a skull with a hole in it which had been found on the site of the battlefield of Marston Moor. The presumed cause of death was the bullet which rattled about in the box in which the skull was kept and which had been found inside the cranium of the deceased. The recipient of the box irreverently nicknamed its contents "Faceless Fred with a bullet in his head". Fred was considered to have been a Cavalier rather than a Roundhead, for the latter's leather helmet would have been likely to protect his head from flying bullets. Therefore, I was reliably informed, a Roundhead skull would have sustained radiating cracks on impact rather than the clean penetration seen here. So it was accepted that Fred was a Cavalier.

Temporarily, he was kept in his box on top of our television, so that the recipient of this macabre legacy could show him to his archaeological acquaintances. Unknown to me, my children displayed Fred and his bullet to their babysitters, who left. Hence, box and contents were banished to a large, walk-in bedroom cupboard.

One night, alone in the house except for the children, I awoke in darkness at about midnight to hear movements from the cupboard. I lay rigid with fright as the noise became louder and more insistent; it was an intermittent knocking from beyond the cupboard door. Something - or someone - was trying to get out! Had the long-dead Cavalier come back to haunt us? Poor Fred! Still scared, but determined to get some sleep, I switched on the light and opened the cupboard door. Out stepped, not Fred, but... our cat!

Had the long-dead Cavalier come back to haunt us ...

Sussex rivals Hampshire in its myths and legends.

An eerie scene

Mr. Norman Keates of 29 Sunningdale Gardens, Bognor, tells me of an oral tradition that "If you walk seven times backwards round a large yew tree in South Bersted churchyard, Sussex, chanting the Lord's Prayer backwards, at midnight on a full moon, the devil is supposed to appear from the tree." He added: "It's a difficult task because there are things in the way such as gravestones."

Recalling an incident when he was much younger, he said he went to this churchyard with a friend one night of full moon, at about 11.50 p.m.

"The weather was fine, clouds rushed across the moon which made the scene eerie. After wandering about the churchyard until nearly twelve, my friend took out his prayer book and torch and commenced walking round the tree backwards, tripping over the odd tombstone on the way. After doing so while saying the Lord's Prayer backwards, we waited for something to happen. Suddenly ... all the streetlights went out! Shocking! My friend had taken some Holy Water with him, 'just in case'." Both youths were terrified, but, as Mr. Keates explained, the street lights always go out at midnight. The lad with the Holy Water was a Catholic; it seems, ironically, the bizarre prank was a demonstration of his faith, for otherwise, there would have been no point in arming himself with Holy Water.

Those tuned in to such things can hear the thud of horses' hooves on the hilltop at Chanctonbury Ring, Sussex, an Iron Age hillfort where no bird sings, so they say, among the innumerable beech trees on the summit and what is more, should anyone succeed in counting the beeches, Julius Caesar and his army will arise. A white-bearded old man who wanders the hilltop whether you count the trees or not is supposed to be the ghost of a Druid ...

If you can add to the above legends from your own region, or can supply a southern counties ghost story from your experience or that of a friend, relative or colleague; if you have seen a flying saucer or had a premonition or talked to a man who isn't there; if your child has an invisible playmate, your horse shies at shadows or your pet seems to know something you don't; even if you thought you met a ghost and

116

then found a perfectly ordinary, unromantic explanation - please write to me, Pat Ross, c/o The King's England Press, 21, Commercial Road, Goldthorpe Industrial Estate, Goldthorpe, Rotherham, South Yorkshire S63 9BL.

I would be particularly pleased to hear from readers from the Southampton area, from the residents of Sussex and from those who can relate stories of the theatre and the armed services. All letters will be answered, and if sufficient stories are received we hope to include them in our next volume.

THANKS My thanks go to all those who have contributed personal stories; to the local press, especially Sandy Jones of Radio Solent; to Chichester Folk Song Club and to Mrs. J. Harckham; to Ron Brown for material from his files; Hampshire County Council Library, especially staff at Winchester and Havant; Winchester Museums Service, especially Mr. K. Qualmann.

REFERENCES

Brode, Anthony. *Haunted Hampshire* (Countryside Books, 1981)

Brooks, John. *The Good Ghost Guide* (Jarrold, 1994)

Brown, Ron. *Down Memory Lane* (Gosport Standard)

Brown, Ron. *The Pubs of Portsmouth* (Milestone, 1984)

Cousins, R. and Rogers, P. *Bygone Havant* (Phillimore, 1993)

"Daily News" article on the Brushmaker's ghost. Upham School Report Project (June 1992)

Evans, Gwladys. "Haunted Inns" from *Hampshire Haunts and Legends* p. 3- 4 (date unknown)

Farquharson-Coe. *Hants and Dorset's Ghosts* (James Pike Ltd., 1975)

"Folklore, Myths and Legends of Great Britain" (*Reader's Digest*, 1977)

Forman, Joan. *The Haunted South* (date unknown)

Fortean Times No. 80, p. 37

Fox, Ian. *The Haunted Places of Hampshire* (Ensign Publications, 1993)

Guille, Rosemary E. *The Guinness Encyclopaedia of Ghosts and Spirits*

Hallam, Jack. *The Haunted Inns of England* (Wolfe Publishing, London, date unknown)

Havant Library files cutting of 20.10.84, probably from The *News*

Linahan, Liz. *Pit Ghosts, Padfeet and Poltergeists* (The King's England Press, 1994)

Morton, H.V.. *In Search of England* (Methuen, 1930 edition)

Russel, Leonard (ed.). *The Saturday Book,* ninth edition (Hutchinson)

Shaw, T.W. *History of Hampshire* (EP Publishing, 1976, reprint of 1892 edition)

Thomas, F.G.S. *The King Holds Hayling* (Concise Editions, 1978, reprint of 1961 edition)

Underwood, Peter. *Ghosts of Hampshire and the Isle of Wight* (St.Michael's Abbey Press, 1983)

Williamson, June. "Rowlands Castle", Hampshire County Library Local History Collection

Winter, C.W.R. *The Manor Houses of the Isle of Wight* (Michael Rainey, 1984)

Index

ILLUSTRATIONS

The line illustrations on pages 52, 59, 66, 74, 90, 94,100, and 115 are by the author.

The photographs on pages 25 and 74 are from the author's collection.

The line illustration on page 26 is by Julie Thompson.

The photographs of Odiham Castle on page 92 and Silchester on page 108 are from *The King's England: Hampshire* by Arthur Mee, to be reprinted by The King's England Press.

All remaining illustrations are believed by the publisher and author to be in the public domain.

DISCLAIMER

The concept of ghosts and of what is popularly known as "The Occult" can be a difficult one for some people to come to terms with. Neither the author nor the publisher can accept any responsibility for any actions whatsoever arising from anyone having read this book. The author and publishers strongly urge those troubled by such matters to seek counselling from a qualified spiritual advisor appropriate to their religious faith.